THE CAR BUYER'S BIBLE

THE CAR BUYER'S BIBLE

FEATURING THE EIGHT COMMANDMENTS FOR BUYING A CAR

ROBIN SEGAL, PH.D.

Murray Hill Books, LLC
220 Madison Avenue
Suite 10H
New York, NY 10016

(212) 689-5232
www.murrayhillbooks.com
info@murrayhillbooks.com
SAN 256-3622

Cover Design by Cathi Stevenson
www.bookcoverexpress.com

Library of Congress Control Number: 2004117428
ISBN 0-9719697-4-4

Table of Contents

Introduction

Philosophy Of This Book

Central to this book is the belief that car dealerships can be fair places, not bad places; that car salesmen, (I use that term for male and female salespeople in this book,) are regular people, not bad people; and that car buyers are well-intentioned but ***undereducated in the skills they need to negotiate a fair deal on a car.***

The price of a car is negotiable. It is up to each side in the transaction to negotiate the best deal possible. The "sale" is simply made when both sides agree. There need not be victims or thieves.

Think of a car dealership as a marketplace, an actual commodity-trading floor. The commodity is the car. Even though you are buying a durable good for yourself, you can look at it the same way you might invest money in a company's stock. After all, you are betting on this car to provide you with a decent return on your investment, even though that return will be made up of a number of elements; good performance, low operating and maintenance costs, and high resale value.

You need to be comfortable with the price at which you buy the commodity. There are many ways to make a decision about making a financial investment. Let us look at these ways according to how much control you have over the price at which you buy. The first, safest but least flexible way to make a financial investment is to buy a mutual fund with a historically decent return. With a mutual fund, you have no power to change the price of the purchase. You can either buy the fund or not. A second way to invest, where you have more power over the price of your investment, is to call your broker, and with his or her guidance, make a buy order if the stock hits a certain price. A third way to invest, where you have the most power over the price you pay for your investment, is to become a day trader and watch the minute-to-minute price fluctuations of the stock that interests you, to master the minutiae of the market, and to be responsive to every nuance of the stock's movement.

Now let us take this analogy into the world of car dealerships. The first, least risky investment model is the mutual fund. Buying a mutual fund is like buying a Saturn. You get the standard Saturn product, with some options or variations. You give up freedom for security. Saturn will make a good profit on the sale of the car to you because you may not negotiate the price down, but Saturn will not make an enormous profit on your car because they may not negotiate the price up. Like a mutual fund, your risk is much less than if you negotiate the price of this investment by yourself. But this option also may yield you a lower return, potentially, than if you had done your research and made winning investment decisions.

The second investment model is the full service broker. In the world of car dealerships, using a car buying service is like buying stock through a well-reputed, full-service broker. You will probably get a pretty good deal, but you would be correct if you suspected that you could do a little better, given a lot more information and time, to research the car market and negotiate the deal yourself.

The third investment model is the day trader. In the world of car dealerships, going down to the dealership in person, and going up against a random salesman, on a random day, is like being a day trader in the financial market, executing your own trades.

Unfortunately, most car buyers think they are entitled to pay a very low price for a car just because they ask for it. They think they are entitled to a rock bottom price, one far, far below sticker price, without working for it. The "work" that buyers need to do falls into two categories: research and negotiation. Under "research," every buyer needs to decide which car he wants, and "how much car," as they say in the business, he can afford. Finding the car he wants is the buyer's favorite part. Determining which car he can afford is more difficult. But the part with which buyers have the most difficult time, and that other buyers' guides do not tackle systematically, is how to negotiate.

Negotiation is a science. Negotiation is an art. There is nothing wrong with negotiation if car buyers realize that every item in the marketplace is in some way negotiated, whether it is by buyers and sellers, or by their agents. There is no universal fair deal. If people suddenly did not want cars anymore, then their retail market price, that is their negotiated price, would drop, simple as that. *This book tells you how to negotiate with confidence.*

By following the eight commandments, or rules, that I set forth in this book, you will become a better negotiator. This book will help you get a fair deal on a car. If you do not want to negotiate, then the best thing to do is to buy a Saturn or hire a car broker to do the work for you. Whichever option you choose, there are trade-offs. Reading this book is the option that affords you the most freedom: the freedom to choose the car you want to buy, and the freedom to negotiate all parts of the deal yourself. Read this book, follow the commandments in it, and you will have the tools you need to negotiate a fair deal on a car.

Format of this Book

The rules I put forth in this book are so important to getting a fair deal on a car that I refer to them as *commandments*. But the real reason I had the audacity to call this book THE CAR BUYER'S BIBLE is because it is an *inspired* guide to buying a car. The "faith" that you need to use this book is the faith that you *can* buy a car at a dealership without getting ripped off, and all you have to do is understand and stick to the commandments in this book. These commandments, together, support the belief that you can get a fair deal on a car in a dealership without hurting anybody, and without getting ripped off.

Once you have finished reading this book, you will *understand* car dealerships. You will have the confidence to go into one and buy a car for a fair price. If you believe it can be done, then after you read this book you will believe that *you* can do it, and then you *will* do it.

Each chapter in this book is about one commandment. Each commandment is explained and illustrated by a series of stories. After you read each chapter, you will understand and appreciate why that chapter's commandment is necessary to guaranteeing you a fair deal on a car. At the end of each chapter is one or more things you should do before you visit the dealership. These "to do" lists are consolidated in one list in the third appendix at the end of the book.

Other books tell you salesmen's tactics, and how to deal with them. Other books guide you to figure out what monthly payments you can afford. This book tells you what you need to enter a negotiation.

These Are the Eight Commandments:

• FIRST COMMANDMENT: BUY THIS BOOK
AND READ IT

• SECOND COMMANDMENT: VISIT YOUR BANK

• THIRD COMMANDMENT: GET EXCITED
ABOUT YOUR FUTURE CAR

• FOURTH COMMANDMENT: BE WILLING
TO WALK AWAY FROM THE SALE

• FIFTH COMMANDMENT: WRITE
DOWN EVERYTHING YOUR SALESMAN SAYS

• SIXTH COMMANDMENT: DO NOT TRY
TO "UNDERSTAND" YOUR SALESMAN

• SEVENTH COMMANDMENT: DO NOT LIE

• EIGHTH COMMANDMENT: NEGOTIATE
EVERY PART OF THE SALE

The first three commandments must be completed before you go to the dealership. That is, you need to have learned what you want to buy, what you can afford to buy, and what to expect *at* the dealership before you go *to* the dealership. That means you need to read this whole book before you visit your car dealership. The dealership is a good place to buy a car, not a good place to learn what your budget is or what you like.

Genesis of this Book

Once upon a time I was a car salesman. I took the job in order to do research for my academic career, not because I wanted to sell cars. I thought I was going to be the only "good" salesperson among a dealership of liars. Turns out most of the liars I met on the job were my customers. The salesmen did very little lying by comparison.

Now, before you get angry and throw this book down, I want to tell you that lying is a natural response to feeling like somebody is taking advantage of you. Most buyers feel like they are at a disadvantage the minute they walk through the dealership door, so they do not hesitate to lie to their salesmen from the outset.

"I'm just looking." "I intend to buy... but not today." These seem like harmless lies, but in fact they tip off the salesman to the fact that the customer is a liar. This gives the salesman, in his mind, license to lie back. And so begins the battle of deceit and manipulation that buyers assume is inevitable.

During the time I sold cars, I learned how to *buy* a car without having to lie even once. The key is to stick to the Eight Commandments . I discovered these commandments the hard way; *by wishing my customers would only follow them!!* You might be able to negotiate a fair deal without following them, but if you follow them all, you will guarantee yourself a fair deal on a car.

Chapter One

THE EIGHT COMMANDMENTS

FIRST COMMANDMENT: BUY THIS BOOK AND READ IT

By reading this book, you are at least considering the possibility that you will be able to negotiate a fair deal on a car, at a car dealership.

You are accepting that there is a positive, fair-minded way to buy a car, that you do not need to reduce yourself to "clever" tactics (that your car salesman knows five ways around anyway).

This First Commandment locks you into all the others. Just as the Bible's First Commandment tells you to have no other God, I am telling you to follow no other system or approach to buying a car- only the system in this book. If you skip some of the commandments, this system will not work for you. The commandments work together. Together, the Eight Commandments in this book are the strategy for getting a fair deal on a car.

It is important to read this book before you do research into your specific car. You need to really understand the commandments as you look for the car you want and assess what you can afford. The rest of this chapter introduces you to the seven other commandments.

SECOND COMMANDMENT: VISIT YOUR BANK

Car salesmen will try to "educate" you on the relative benefits of leasing and financing your new car. The best way to learn your best options, based on your credit history, with regard to your desired car and your other expenses and income is to get individual attention, not some sales pitch from a salesman who does not know very much about finance and even less about you. The best place to get this attention and to ask questions and get honest, straight answers, is your bank, preferably a non-commercial bank such as a Savings and Loan, or a credit union.

I could explain all of the financing options to you, but the bottom line is that the bottom line is different for each buyer. Don't trust your car salesman to educate you- he's trying to sell you a car *and* the financing. Your personal banker will only try to sell you a loan and, unlike some dealerships, will not want you to default on that loan.

It is well known that in car sales, dealerships make the greatest profit on the financing portion of the sale, not on the "price" you pay for the car.

In the rare event that you are sure you are going to pay cash for your car, you do not need to talk to your banker. However, it is a good idea to talk to your banker anyway, if for no other reason than to familiarize yourself with which financing options you qualify for, in case you change your mind.

Chapter Two and the Second Commandment look at the way salesmen lie to take your money in financing deals more successfully than they lie and profit on any other part of the sale. Reading this chapter should frighten you over to your bank very quickly.

THIRD COMMANDMENT: GET EXCITED ABOUT YOUR FUTURE CAR

Desire is a big part of American car culture. Face it, cars are fun and desirable. It is better to come to terms with this before the salesman starts waxing poetic about how you are "gonna fall in love with this car." Even if you are a stoic, unwilling car shopper, enjoy choosing your car and imagining all the pleasures driving it and owning it will bring you. As much as we like to think we are dispassionate about buying cars, we Americans are very passionate about owning our cars. If you deny yourself the excitement about your future car, your salesman will get you excited about it and you will lose focus when you visit the dealership.

Chapter Three and the Third Commandment is about the way car salesmen, and the car industry generally, use sexual imagery and other methods of seduction to sell cars. Enjoy it in privacy and get it out of your system. Then beware of it at the dealership.

FOURTH COMMANDMENT: BE WILLING TO WALK AWAY FROM THE SALE

In some sales situations, the *only* possible deal is a bad deal, and you should *never* settle for a bad deal. The Fourth Commandment teaches that you can negotiate a fair deal, but that you cannot force a determined crooked salesman to go straight with you. Sometimes you meet a rotten apple and the best and *only* thing to do is to find a different apple.

The central principle of Chapter Four and the Fourth Commandment is that there is more than one place to buy the car you want. Salesmen employ pressure tactics because they face competition, more often than not right down the street. If you follow all of the other commandments and still can't get a fair deal, go somewhere else.

FIFTH COMMANDMENT: WRITE DOWN EVERYTHING YOUR SALESMAN SAYS

Bring a notebook to the dealership and write down everything about the car and about the deal. Write everything in your own words so that you are sure you understand all the information flowing from the salesman to you. The Fifth Commandment is all about staying in control. You do this by not losing your confidence. If everything your salesman says goes into your notebook, in your own words, then you can *always* refer to it later on, even if the information leaves your brain as soon as you write it down. Take your time. Repeat what the salesman says. Ask for clarification as often as you have to. Many very smart people pretend they understand the terms of a deal when they do not understand because they think they look stupid if they admit that something is unclear to them. More often than not, the salesman wants to keep you confused in order to be able to change the terms of the deal on you. Don't let him. Your best defense is the clarity of a perfect written record; a record of what is offered to you. Write everything down and keep looking at your notes. Do not let yourself be rushed; dealerships will gladly remain open until the middle of the night if they think they are going to sell you a car.

Chapter Five and the Fifth Commandment is about the way salesmen mislead, distract, avoid, hurry the sale, or slow down the sale, all in an effort to destabilize, distract, and confuse the customer. You will see, as you read about all of these tactics, that if you keep a perfect written record of what is said between you and the salesman, you will disarm the salesman of his advantage. An advantage gained, by the way, from extensive experience negotiating car sales every day. Experience you do not have.

SIXTH COMMANDMENT: DO NOT TRY TO "UNDERSTAND" YOUR SALESMAN

Do not try to "understand" your salesman. You will not. Car salesmen are very strange people. And they are very creative. To succeed at sales, salesmen must be natural psychologists. They will probably understand you better than you will ever understand them. You cannot guess what they will do next, and trying will only distract you from the sale.

Chapter Six tells you the type of people who become car salesmen, why, what they are taught, and what they think they are doing. The moral of these stories is that most car salesmen's minds are scary places and you should not want to share, understand, or even entertain their versions of reality. Stay focused on the car and the deal.

SEVENTH COMMANDMENT: DO NOT LIE

Most people think car salesmen lie all the time. They don't. Stay anchored in the truth when you negotiate. You will have more self-confidence and be more difficult to outsmart.

EIGHTH COMMANDMENT: NEGOTIATE EVERY PART OF THE SALE

Most buyers think that the "price" of the car is the only negotiable part of the sale. You know from the Second Commandment (Visit Your Bank) that all financing packages accrue huge profits to the dealership. So too with options and aftermarket. And why can't service contracts and parts be negotiable? Also, manufacturers are always giving dealerships great financial incentives to move certain cars off their lots. Ask about these "manufacturer to dealer incentives." Not only might it save you money if you ask, but your salesman will think you are savvy, which you are.

Chapter Eight and the Eighth Commandment is about the ways salesmen profit on the sale of a single car. It will wake you up to the opportunity that exists for you to save more money than by simply demanding a discount off "sticker price." Don't spend all your effort trying to buy a car for "$100 below dealer invoice" and then paying a huge markup on accessories. The better you understand the industry, the more money you can save. Chapter Eight and the Eighth Commandment tell you how to look for savings at many points throughout the sale.

First Commandment - To Do:

♦ Buy this book and read the whole thing!

Chapter Two

SECOND COMMANDMENT: VISIT YOUR BANK BEFORE YOU VISIT THE DEALERSHIP

Car salesmen will try to "educate" you on the relative benefits of leasing and financing your new car. The best way to learn *your* best options, based on *your* credit history, with regard to *your* desired car and *your* other expenses and income is to get individual attention, not some sales pitch from a salesman who does not know very much about finance and even less about you. The best place to get this attention and to ask questions and get honest, straight answers, is your non-commercial bank or credit union. Credit unions are nonprofit, cooperative financial institutions owned and run by their members. They are democratically controlled institutions that provides their members with a safe place to save and borrow money at rates that are usually lower than bank rates or other commercial institution loan rates. However, you need to be a member in order to get a car loan from a credit union. Many employers, unions, and community organizations have credit unions. If you are a member already, check out their car loans. If you are not a member, see if you qualify to join one. The resource guide at the end of this book has websites you can consult to find credit unions all over the United States.

Wherever you end up securing a car loan, you will probably have several financing options. I could explain all of the financing options to you in this book, but that would be overkill. A car buyer only needs detailed information on a given financing option if that is the option that best suits his needs. In other words, the bottom line is that the bottom line is *different* for each buyer. Don't trust your car salesman to educate you on all the options he says are available to you- he's trying to confuse you, *and* he is trying to sell you a car *and* financing. Your personal banker will *only* try to sell you a loan and, unlike some dealerships, will not *want* you to default on that loan.

It is well known that in car sales, dealerships make the greatest profit on the financing portion of the sale, not primarily on the "price" you pay for the car.

Salesmen lie to take your money in financing deals more successfully than they lie and profit on any other part of the sale. There are, to be sure, exceptions to this rule. Car manufacturers offer very good financing from time to time, but if you opt for it, be very careful because there can be contingencies such as requirements to purchase an extended warranty, or credit insurance, or many other add-ons that end up making the "low" rate not so low in the end.

Where I sold cars, like at many dealerships, each salesman's desk displayed a laminated cardboard flip chart explaining the three available payment options. Salesmen were "allowed" to answer customers' questions about these three general schemes, but nothing more. The first page on the flip chart was about buying the car outright. That's simple enough, and also rare enough. The second page was about financing the car, that is, one lump payment at the beginning, and then many small payments for a fixed term such as two years or five years. The third page was about leasing. Leasing means lots of small payments for three years, then one big payment at the end... or no big payment at the end. That is how it is presented in the flip chart... Salesmen were supposed to push customers to opt for the plan containing *no big payments at all,* simply on the appeal of "no big payments." Some customers resonated to this implication, not thinking, of course, that the balloon payment at end of the lease term is the mechanism by which they get to keep the car forever. As astounding as it sounds, confused shoppers sometimes overlooked the fact that buying and financing a car resulted in owning the car, while leasing the car for a fixed term did not.

It is important to note that leasing laws vary by state. When you lease a car, you do not own it. Who is responsible for the damage when the car is in an accident is the subject of many disputes , as you can imagine, and the laws governing the outcomes of these disputes vary by state. Your dealership will not advise you whether it is wise to lease in your state. Your bank will help you with this issue, and may advise you to get a loan with a balloon payment at the end instead of a lease.

The real art of getting a person to pay at car dealerships is saved for the finance box, and the finance box is saved until after the salesman and customer "shake hands" on the deal. This makes no sense, but this is exactly how many dealerships operate.

Even if you are not planning to finance or lease the car, go to your bank or credit union and ask about getting a car loan. Learn what you can afford, according to the bank, so that when you go to the dealership, you will already know. While at the bank, ask about the advertised car dealership financing in the newspaper you "happen to" have with you. A banker will explain how car loans and leasing work. Fill out a credit application. Better to get the bad news about what you can afford from the bank. The bank will try to sell you a loan, but it is not as interested as the car dealership, which will try to sell you a loan *and* a car.

SCAMS

Here is a true story about a car dealership finance scam: There is a certain dealership that sells used cars and caters to a generally poor clientele. And there is a finance company. The guy who owns the dealership also owns half of the finance company. The dealership sells used cars, with the customers financing them through this finance company at the maximum rate allowed by law. On any given deal, the customer might make a couple of payments and then default. This would happen because the dealership would take as much cash as they could for the down payment. They might tell the customer: "You have bad credit, so you must give us five thousand dollars up front," some amount that would put the customer in such financial trouble that he would almost certainly default on his payments. Sooner or later, more often sooner, the car is repossessed, and the finance company turns around and sells the car at "auction." But no one ever comes to these auctions, except the dealership that sold the cars originally. As per the legal requirement, the finance company would put an ad in the paper announcing the time and place of the auction, but nobody would ever come to the auction because everybody in the trade knew that the car was going to be sold back to the original dealership, and it would end up back on the dealership lot, to be resold for another profit.

The finance company then could sue the customer to cover the deficiency, that is, to recover the payments that it allegedly lost in the deal. If the loan was for twelve thousand dollars, for example, but the car is only worth five thousand, the finance company would sell it back at public auction to the car dealership for five, but the customer still would owe seven thousand dollars on the loan. The customer is now without a car *and* in debt to the finance company. The dealership sucked up all the cash they could by getting as large a down payment as possible for two reasons. One, it puts money in their pocket, and two, it makes it more likely the customer will default on the loan.

Defaulting on a loan can be the result of an unfortunate, un-planned event. It can also be finely tuned to happen by a crooked finance company, particularly one that is used to financing cars for people who have never made a large installment purchase and who have not yet developed the savvy to manage their own finances.

Of course not all dealerships and finance companies operate crookedly, but the number that do employ illegal or other unfair tactics is certainly not zero. And so, while you may be clever enough to detect a dealership finance man who is trying to get you to sign for a twelve thousand dollar loan on a five thousand dollar pur-chase, finance in general is very complicated. It is *much* more likely that you will be lied to during the finance part of the sale, after you shake hands with your salesman on a "purchase price" deal.

The dealership finance man might tell you that you need full insurance coverage on your car in order to qualify for the loan in question. He might tell you that you need to purchase a service contract, even life insurance. These are serious lies, and custom-ers rarely detect them. Lenders virtually never require borrowers to purchase such supplemental policies – the vehicle is adequate collateral for the loan. If lenders do require borrowers to purchase more than just financing, the law usually requires that these charg-es be disclosed as part of the finance charge. Consumer protection legislation covering this area is meant to let consumers shop around for credit. If dealerships sell disability, life, or medical insurance, or a service contract, the deal becomes very profitable.

A consumer protection attorney told me this:

> What you see when you look at the fine print: 'I understand that this is optional.' That's what it says, in writing. But in fact, as you know, when you're in the

closing room with this big, burly guy, he says, 'You want the car, you gotta buy this, because the lender has to be protected.' And most people say, 'OK,' and they sign it. So, even though the contract says it's optional, it's not. I mean people are told something very different from what the paper says. It's a total charade. The reality is the usury laws and the truth in lending laws are being broken all the time. All the time. The real problem in a dealership is in the back end of the deal.

The best way for you to avoid all of this is to never step into the "finance box" in the first place.   Visit your non-commercial bank or credit union, talk to your banker or credit union officer, and get a car loan from them.   Then go to the dealership and make a deal on the car's purchase price. *Do not make a "monthly payments" deal* without understanding *exactly* your deal's principle, interest rate, down payment, frees, and term of loan. The chances of getting the best or even a good financing deal on a car from a dealership are very, very slim.

What about buying a Saturn, you might be wondering. In a Saturn dealership, *only* the "purchase price" of the car is fixed... at somewhere in the neighborhood of ten percent above dealer invoice. Financing a Saturn is fraught with the same perils as financing any other brand or make of car.

If you think you can do better than paying about ten percent above dealer invoice for a Saturn, particularly if you do not want a Saturn to begin with, then visit your bank and learn what you can afford.

SECOND COMMANDMENT – TO DO

◆ Have a general idea of the car you want to buy, but be flexible.

◆ See if you can join a credit union. If so, join. If not, make an appointment with your personal banker.

◆ Ask your credit union officer or banker to explain to you what it would cost you, up front and over time, to:

(1)   Buy the car outright, with cash, if you can afford it;

(2)   Get a loan from your bank to buy the car, either a traditional loan or one with a balloon payment at the end;

(3)   Take the dealership loan advertised in your local newspaper;

(4)   Lease the car. You need to know the lease term, the monthly payments, and your options at the end of the leasing term.

Chapter Three

THIRD COMMANDMENT: GET EXCITED ABOUT YOUR FUTURE CAR

Desire is a big part of American car culture. Face it, cars are fun and desirable. It is better to come to terms with this *before* the salesman starts waxing poetic about how you are "gonna *fall in love* with this car." Even if you are a stoic, unwilling car shopper, enjoy choosing your car and imagining all the pleasures driving it and owning it will bring you. As much as we like to think we are dispassionate about buying cars, we Americans are very passionate about owning our cars. If you deny yourself the excitement about your future car, your salesman will get you excited about it and you will lose focus when you visit the dealership.

This chapter is about the way car salesmen, and the car industry generally, use sexual imagery and other methods of seduction to sell cars. Enjoy it in privacy and get it out of your system. Then beware of it at the dealership.

WHEN MEN ARE FROM MAZDA AND WOMEN ARE FROM VEGAS

What is the nature of car sales? What are car salesman doing to us when they try to sell us cars? I thought about this for a very long time. I entertained all of the theories, but in the end, I accepted the most obvious.

The year was 1996. As my airport shuttle bus rattled through the neon streets of Las Vegas towards the National Automobile Dealers Association annual convention, Mayor Jan Lafferty-Jones welcomed us to her enticing city from inside a mounted, on-board TV monitor. Jan Lafferty-Jones is no stranger to car dealers or to television. She rose to the pinnacle of Las Vegas politics through a successful televised career advertising for her husband Fletcher Jones' car dealership empire. Since popular perceptions of car dealers, casino owners, prostitutes and local politicians often sulk together below the bottom rung on the ladder of respectable professions, it seems natural for Las Vegas to have elected an attractive, charismatic car dealer to run its affairs. Car salesmen are blamed for their selling "tricks," much as fast, dangerous, (and often highly profitable women are blamed for the phenomenon of sexual prostitution, even though all prostitution requires sellers *and* buyers.

Wait a minute. Comparing car sales to prostitution is radical and unfair. After all, selling cars is a legal and important part of one of America's largest industries, and prostitution is illegal. But a broader definition of prostitution is "to put one's talent or ability to unworthy use." In this sense, people in many professions prostitute themselves, and no profession is more notoriously full of shameful and demeaning acts than car sales. In the car trade and the sex trade, all but perhaps the highest caliber sellers are commonly regarded as desperate people who do demeaning things for a living.

Demeaning or not, many who work in car sales and prostitution win business by selling their customers a fantasy. Like the fantasy packaged in sex for sale, it is the fantasy in the desire for cars (as opposed to the fulfillment of personal transportation needs) that have shaped the sleazy image of the American car selling industry. But there is one big difference. In selling sex, the and the product are the same thing. In car sales, the product is the car, and the advertising is spread among newspapers, television, radio, billboards, the cars on the street, and the glossy brochures we're slapped with at the dealership. Car salesmen are really only the final and most direct advertising, the human incarnation of the glossy brochure. "Love this car! Buy this car!"

The car business and the sex business work at similar paces and rhythms. Most people drift in and out of the professions, but some really find their groove and make a career of it. They adjust. Both businesses are not fast or slow, but periods of intensity burst forth amid long hours of waiting. During the waiting, car sales-men accomplish a lot. They motivate themselves. They have to, or else they'll lose their energy. During the down time, salesmen tell stories, spin schemes and wrap them around their hands, and when customers approach, they wave their hands, and the schemes un-ravel into car fantasies before the customers' eyes. These fantasies, played out in duet by the buyer's desire and the salesman's motiva-tion is, according to the veterans in this business, what sell cars.

In the beginning, when I approached customers at the car dealership, they always seemed to be intelligent, thoughtful, and rational, but they did not buy many cars from me. Perhaps if my rational and calm approach "worked," it worked to dissuade peo-ple from buying cars, and persuaded them to think more clearly about the cars they really needed, and less about the romance in the moment. At the time, I did not understand the central place and power of fantasy. If Jimmy Jeffries, my sales trainer and manager, had told me that I was just a car whore, I think I would have either quit immediately or been very, very successful.

Comparing prostitution and car salesmanship is not exactly intuitive. In prostitution, the fall of righteous man in the arms of the whore, the temptress, creates a powerful image that underlies our common cultural demonization of prostitution. Yet, we have as a culture informally relegated the car salesman to the same immoral, unsavory category and portrayed the car buyer as an innocent dupe. When we buy cars, we expect to fulfill our fantasies by seeking rational action, and this mismatch of fantastic expectations and ordinary means promises nothing less than tragedy in the classic sense. A car salesman's job is to see the real fantasy behind the car talk, and then to set the appropriate romantic mood during the customer-car courtship. That is, actually, his job. How do car salesmen know what customers need, both practically and in their dreams? The predictably high drama between car buyers and car sellers can take on a myriad of fantastic qualities, but most important is that it is almost always a drama precisely because so much of it is based in fantasy of one kind or another.

As best-selling "relationships" author John Gray has noted many times in many books, men and women are indeed creatures from different planets when it comes to romance. Since cars are about romance and, for the most part, men sell cars, obviously men and women respond differently to "the selling system." In the car-shopping event itself, women tend not to respond to car salesmen's pressure tactics or the mean spirited negotiation forced upon them. Yet, the overwhelming trend in automobile selling still caters to men's desire to find, pursue, and capture their objects of desire, that is to purchase cars through spot negotiation in a high-pressure environment.

DIVORCED FROM REALITY

Imagine what it is like to sell a car to a person who is lukewarm on the concept of buying a new car, but very heavily invested in trying to escape his unpleasant reality... Many events in our lives prompt us to seek material change in an attempt to explore and reflect on our inner changes. But with the frontal strike of divorce, people tread the rough seas of each day searching for "answers." If the answers cannot be found in prescriptive self-help books, perhaps they are hiding behind the wheel of a shiny new sports car. Especially if you are prompted to buy a car to celebrate or distract yourself from a life-changing event, it is very important not to get lost in fantasy when you are at the dealership. Salesmen can smell the mid-life crisis avoidance fantasy a mile away, and they know how to play with it. When I met up with it for the first time, I simply couldn't believe it. I was a salesman who handled it wrong. My customer was lucky.

At about eleven o'clock on one of my first mornings selling cars, an attractive middle-aged man, whose name I later learned was Franco, drove up in a middle-aged sedan. Franco was bright-eyed and interested in the stock, but I doubted whether he looked like the frequent car trade-in type. Before I was able to peg him, learn his story, or even smell the nature of his desire to buy, we were test-driving a car. Franco seemed so happy to be in this car and out of his, and he extended his test drive well beyond the five or ten or even fifteen minutes normally required to get the feel of the car. Finally, Franco spoke frankly. Years ago, his wife had purchased the car that was waiting for him back at the dealership. He told me this matter-of-factly. Then he added even more matter-of-factly, "And then she decided she didn't want to be my wife anymore." Silence. More silence. The last thing I wanted to do was encourage him, though in retrospect, that is exactly what I should have done to sell him the car. Franco's wife had left him with the car... and the car payments. Franco stunned me with this information. I didn't understand why he was telling *me*. Then I realized that he just needed to tell his car salesman. Car salesmen are drawn into personal dramas like this one every day, as confidants, as psychologists. Customers in crisis invite car salesmen into their emotions, hoping that the salesmen will patch up their wounds with shiny, red, $25,000 band-aids. When you, the reader, finish reading this book and go out to shop for a car, *do not do that*. Your salesman, if he is half decent, will use it against you.

But now back to the story of Franco. When we returned to the dealership, the time was a quarter to noon, and Franco smiled at me with the smile that says, "I'm having such fun, aren't you?" He suggested that we talk about the sale over lunch. I stood there in silence, emotionally flipped out by this suggestion. I realized then that Franco not only needed me to understand him and sell him a car; he also needed me to play romantic co-star to help him get beyond his ex-wife. Lunch was way beyond my professional comfort level. While this was not a serious or lasting dilemma for me, it caught me off-guard. Not only did I decline lunch with Franco, I also stopped trying to sell him a car. I guess I just froze, so surprised at the power of the car to attract and thrust people out of their problems, that I could barely speak as I gave him my card and waved him goodbye.

I was immediately installed in a manager's office. Behind a slammed door, I withstood a harsh lecture about the central place of role-playing in car salesmanship. Still amazed at how strangely cliched my day had been so far, I retreated to a corner of the dealership to reflect on the way people's behavior changes so shamelessly and radically when they are searching for access to whatever type of desire they need to motivate themselves to buy a car.

The vast majority of car salesmen, and all *good* car salesmen, would have capitalized on Franco's desire and used it to sell him a car on the spot. You will almost certainly encounter salesmen who will take advantage of your enthusiasm for your future car, no matter how realistic or appropriate that enthusiasm is, so be sure to put your expansive emotions aside before you walk into the dealership.

THIRD COMMANDMENT - TO DO

◆ Dream about your car. Get brochures. Look at websites. Do a test drive at a dealership where you are absolutely sure you will not buy the car. ENJOY the idea that you will soon have a beautiful new car. This is a very important step. Do not skip it.

Chapter Four

FOURTH COMMANDMENT: BE WILLING TO WALK AWAY FROM THE SALE

In some sales situations, the *only* possible deal is a bad deal, and you should *never* settle for a bad deal. The Fourth Commandment teaches that you can negotiate a fair deal, but that you cannot force a determined crooked salesman to go straight with you. Sometimes you meet a rotten apple and the best and only thing to do is to find a different apple.

The central principle of the Fourth Commandment is that there is more than one place to buy the car you want. Salesmen employ pressure tactics because they face competition, more often than not right down the street. If you follow all of the other commandments and still can't get a fair deal, go somewhere else.

MAKING A DEAL WITH MONTY

This is a story about my discovering the Fourth Commandment. Many years ago, I lived in Los Angeles and drove a ten-year old, white VW Rabbit convertible. I loved my topless bunny buggy, but it feigned fatal electrocution too often to be considered endearing. In Los Angeles, city of sprawl with no mass transit, this situation is unacceptable. It was time for a first in my life: a brand new car. I didn't want to think about it, not exactly eager to spend my time thinking about which boring but functional family sedan

I'd end up with upon waving goodbye to $20,000. My husband and I were not really "into" cars. One Saturday morning we resolved to go car shopping, and although we lived within walking distance of a strip of car dealerships, we decided to drive so that we could make a quick getaway, if necessary. We expected unpleasant pressure tactics.

Upon arrival at one of the largest car dealership chains in Southern California, we met a salesman who called himself Monty. With leathery tanned skin from standing in the sun all day, a big, gold chain around his neck, and an open shirt intended to make him seem hipper than his graying pompadour suggested, he was the classic car salesman. If the weather had been cooler, I'm sure his sport coat would have been a barf-colored check. Still, I couldn't help liking him. He was upbeat, and he got me interested in the cars despite the scorching sun and annoyingly loud music.

Until we met Monty, I had been indifferent about our future car, as long as it met our needs and was not too expensive. But after I learned that Monty was from Canada, like me, (or so he said,) the experience got more personal. We shmoozed. Monty started to seem like some pathetic relative, the typical older Jewish, retired, Canada goose, one of a million of that northern flock who fly down to Southern California to live out the rest of their days, away from Canada's eternal winter.

After quite some time kicking around the blacktop full of new cars, we chose a model to test drive. Diligently, Monty skipped off down the burning lot and in a few minutes pulled up in a pre-cooled sedan. While we test drove the car, Monty sat relatively quietly in the back seat, sensing that we did not want his encouragement. We inspected the car, as Monty stood by respectfully, allowing us all the time we needed. Monty was beginning to seem like a reasonable human being after all. My husband and I talked, considered our options, and then agreed on a price with Monty. It was a very low, very good price, partly because of a factory-to-dealer incentive that expired at the end of the day. Monty wanted to make quota. We wanted a good car at a great price. Everybody was happy. We started filling out the reams of paperwork, which were ample because we wanted to finance about half the price of the car.

What happened next was all too typical. Through a glass partition that separated the main showroom from the manager's office, we could see that Monty was mildly disturbed about something. Soon he was visibly "arguing" with his manager. Monty came back, sat down, and frowned. He told us that although we had agreed on a price of $17,000, he could not sell us the car for less than $18,000. He said something about how it was the last day of the sale, and a Sunday, so he could not verify whether we could get that last thousand dollars in a rebate from the manufacturer. We would have to take our chances and be willing to pay $18,000. He pointed out that if we waited, the price would certainly be higher the next day, after the sale ended.

I'm not particularly annoyed by discourtesy or aggression, but I hate being taken for a fool. My reaction to Monty's tactic was immediate and instinctual. I stood up, gave Monty the glare of death, and walked out of his cubicle, leaving my poor husband behind. I walked straight to our ailing VW Rabbit, drove up to the showroom door, revved the engine, and waited. My husband understood me well enough to know that Monty would not be doing business with us that day or any day, and his only option was to get in the car and drive away with me.

Monty didn't know what hit him. We should have been such an easy mark, a naive looking couple in our twenties, dressed in jeans and T-shirts, driving a twelve-year-old car that was obviously loved but in need of replacement by a more "serious" vehicle. We were supposed to have been the kind of customers salesmen love. But in a minute, after Monty attempted to take an additional thousand dollars from us, he lost us, and wasted three hours of his time during a big promotional sales event, while he could have been selling a car to somebody else. Monty stood still, staring after us as we drove away. I stared back through the rearview mirror as he receded into the nasty prologue of car salesman history.

Two miles east and five minutes later, my husband and I walked into another dealership. It was 5 p.m., one hour before closing. It seemed ridiculously late to be shopping for a car, but we were motivated by vengeance on Monty. I approached the salesman, clutching a crumpled newspaper ad, and dared him, as if threatening, "Make-a-Deal-Monty over at your competition tried to rip us off, so we got up and walked out after spending three hours with him. Will you honor this ad and sell us this car, in red, for seventeen thousand dollars?" The salesman seemed used to customers like me. He stared back at me, unblinking. I had been transformed from the customer salesmen must romance all afternoon to the kind of customer with whom salesmen hammer out a deal in two hours without a gesture of warmth, without a smile, without any hype whatsoever. In other words, I had become the customer salesmen *love*. I had been baptized into the highly emotional and volatile world of car sales by the fire of my wrath towards Monty. At 7 p.m. that evening, as we were driving the new car home, I got excited at the prospect of driving by Monty's dealership to wave and taunt him with our day's victory, our trophy, our new car. But my husband urged compassion, so we drove straight home.

I thought about Monty for a long time. What hurt Monty's potential sale to me was not reproach, objection, convulsive yelling, or attempted con-artistry. No, salesmen thrive on that stuff. What hurt him was watching me walk silently out the door, knowing that my husband had no choice but to follow. I left him no handle, no opportunity, no access to me. Monty never saw me again.

My saga with Monty, and the dealership down the street from

his, represents the classic American car buying experience. In the end, I got a good deal, but at the price of my good humor, patience, and open-mindedness about car dealerships and car salesmen. It didn't really bother me, though. After all, the next time I needed to buy a new car, I would expect to do battle with a lying, cheating, sleazy Monty, all over again. I would be prepared.

But then I became a car salesman myself, and I saw the other side of the bargaining table. After several months selling cars, I wrote the Eight Commandments for buying a car. My goal was to develop a system for buyers that results in a fair deal for *both* car buyer and car salesman. I *had to* figure out a way, because I knew both sides of the battle, and I *refused* to believe that there was no way to reconcile the blame heaped upon each side by the other.

IT'S ALL RELATIVE

In reading the story about my deal gone bad with Monty, did you think there was another way to hammer out a deal with Monty? Do you think I could have done something differently, that I could have said something I did not say, or not said something I did say? You might be right. The point of this story is *not* that I did the right thing, or that I knew I'd get the deal I wanted down the street with no hassle at all. The point of the story is that I tried everything I knew how to do, and when I was finished trying everything I knew to negotiate a fair deal, I left the sale. It is important to note that each car buyer is unique. Car buyer guides usually make the mistake of being too prescriptive, assuming that every car buyer will be capable of doing what the author tells them to do in any given situation. This is naïve. All you can do is your best, and your best might be very, very good in one area, and not so good in another area. For example, you might be very, very patient. You might be able to wear the salesman down simply by not being in a hurry. Or, you might be extremely good at talking other people into your proposals, that is, you are good at selling your ideas, just like a car salesman. Whatever your strength, go with it. But whatever your weakness, do not let it force you into an unfair deal. Eventually, you will find a salesman in a dealership who will sell you a car at a fair price.

If, in the end, you realize that you will end up being ripped off just because you hate bargaining, then it is time to consider hiring a car broker. You can look at a car broker as a person who earns some of the money he or she will save you, that you would otherwise have to pay the dealership. That is a perfectly reasonable plan of action. I used a car broker to buy a used car once. It was at a time in my life when I did not have the energy, desire or interest to shop for a used car myself. The car broker was brilliant. On the test drive, she bought us fresh apple turnovers from her "favorite" local bakery. This was the equivalent strategy to a real estate agent baking apples in the oven while holding an open house. I knew what she was doing, but I did not care. In fact, I admired her for it. She sensed that what was important to me at that point in my life was being taken care of, and I sure was willing to pay for that luxury. I bought the car, for a fair brokered price, which was a little more than what I would have paid for it without the services of the broker, but I was very happy with the outcome.

Remember, every price is a negotiated price. The salesman and you need to agree on a price- that is obvious. But you also need to be happy with the price you commit to pay. If it feels like a fair deal, it probably is. If it feels unfair, move on to another dealership or try something else to bring the price down to what you think is fair.

FOURTH COMMANDMENT - TO DO

• Make a list of all the dealerships that could possibly sell you the car you want. Decide how far you are willing to travel to buy this car. In some areas it is a few blocks, and in some many miles. It is up to you. Having a list of more than one dealership (and their hours of business) will make you feel as though you can walk away if you are treated very poorly at any one dealership.

Chapter Five

FIFTH COMMANDMENT: WRITE DOWN EVERYTHING YOUR SALESMAN SAYS

What happens when career automotive snake oil salesmen collide with all-American consumers in a dealership car lot packed to the fence with sexy new minivans, convertibles, and muscle-mobiles? For one thing, consumers get real excited. Desire drives their shopping expeditions as they tempt themselves with new cars and jump through invented hoops in order to justify buying a nicer car than they need. Salesmen stand back, taking customers' psychic pulses and reading their emotional thermometers. The salesman's basic function is to encourage the customer's every positive impulse. We covered the role of desire in American car buying culture in Chapter Three (and Commandment Three: Let yourself desire your car.) But, no matter how in control you think you are once you do enter the dealership, the salesman will be watching you, picking up information about you and using it to take your money. That is his job. Where does that leave you? At a disadvantage, that's where. You need a method to keep control of what is said and promised, between the salesman and you. That brings us to the Fifth Commandment.

Bring a notebook to the dealership and write down everything, about the car, and about the deal. Write everything in your own words so that you are sure you understand all the information flowing from the salesman to you. The Fifth Commandment is all about staying in control. You do this by not losing your confidence. If everything your salesman says goes into your notebook, in your own words, then you can always refer to it later on, even if the information leaves your brain as soon as you write it down. Take your time. Repeat what the salesman says. Ask for clarification as often as you have to. Many very smart people pretend they understand the terms of a deal when they do not understand because they think they look stupid if they admit that something is unclear to them. More often than not, the salesman wants to keep you confused in order to be able to change the terms of the deal on you. Don't let him.

Your best defense is the clarity of a perfect record; a record of what is offered to you. Write everything down and keep looking at your notes. If you write down everything, and I mean everything, salesmen will have a much harder time changing prices and conditions on you. If you keep a record of the things they say, they lose some of the precious control that they rely on to run circles around you and close you in to signing on the line. Use your notebook as a security device... simply don't commit until everything is written down in *your* book, the way *you* understand it. Doing this will slow down the sale when *you* want it to slow down. This tactic will drive your salesman absolutely crazy. Do not let yourself be rushed; dealerships will stay open until the middle of the night if they think they are going to sell you a car.

Chapter Five and the Fifth Commandment are about the way salesmen figure out who you are, and with that information, mislead, distract, avoid, hurry the sale, or slow down the sale, all in an effort to destabilize, distract, and confuse you. You will see, as you read about all of these tactics, that if you keep perfect records of what is said between you and the salesman, you will disarm the salesman of his advantage.

WHAT SALESMEN KNOW ABOUT THEIR CUSTOMERS...

Most of this chapter explains which (and how very much) information salesmen gather about customers without customers suspecting a thing. Why? Who cares what salesmen know about you? You should care. The more your salesman knows about you, the better he will be at overcoming your objections to the sale, once you have started to object to his initial offer. There is no way you can compete with the salesman; you are busy getting to know your future car, and you are busy learning the elements of the deal the salesman is dropping here and there into your "casual" conversation.

The information in the rest of this chapter is intended to scare you. I share this information with you to make the case that you need to be just as, if not more, vigilant and record every piece of relevant information about the car and about the deal, that your salesman tells you. Most buyers believe that the critical time to be vigilant is during the price negotiation. You actually have to start being vigilant as soon as you drive onto the dealership lot.

#1 THE THREE CUSTOMER WALKS

The variety of telltale signs blatantly displayed by each customer is infinite. One of the most amusing and commonly mocked are the customer "walks," each of which normally reveals the customer's overall intention. First, there is the service department customer walk. Everything about this customer is characterized by directness. They even drive onto the lot faster and with a more businesslike character. They don't look out of their car windows as they drive up, and they tend to park anywhere, not specifically in the designated service customer parking spaces. Their cars are more likely to screech to a halt, their doors to fly open. They don't take notice of salesmen approaching as they step out of their cars. Often, they reveal their service tickets, sometimes even deliberately, to ward off the approaching pack of hungry salesmen. Once they leave the safety of their cars, their walks are determined. It is often possible to detect a hint of gloating on their faces, as they note approaching salesmen catch on to the fact that they will not be bringing their business to the sales department. However, the joke is on them since dealerships earn greater profits on parts and service than on new car sales. (*That* topic is covered under the Eighth Commandment.)

The other two customer categories are browsers and buyers. The car buyer's walk resembles the late night walk from the marginal neighborhood outdoor cash machine to the car. It is not as direct as the service customer's walk, but it is decidedly determined, the "don't mess with me" walk. Not a dawdle, not a stride, but mildly concerned. The better the buyer's walk, the more nonchalant it looks. Buyers also feign interest in specific car features. They might stand perfectly still, gazing at a window sticker with finger pointing at the list of features, frozen in fear of the lurking salesman. They tell themselves that by appearing to study the car features window sticker, they might scare the salesman into thinking they know something, that he might have to answer their tough questions, as though they might stump him and gain the upper hand in the sale. Since determined buyers know they will have to interact with salesmen sooner or later, they want to make certain that all the salesmen notice the extent to which they are capable of buying their car with absolutely no help at all.

True browsers walk very, very, slowly, often with hands in pockets. They look a little too nervous to be nervous buyers, but they are just nervous enough to reveal what they know they will bring about: salesmen's badgering and eventual frustration with their absence of buying intention.

#2 MEANS, NEEDS, AND DESIRES

Now the customer is inside and it's time to sell. First there's the requisite, "Hi, how are you!" It is an exclamation, not a question, and then there's the customer's predictable brush off. That's about as far as the script goes. To a salesman, a customer is a sensitive time bomb of means, needs, and desires, and they all must be satisfied to whatever extent they figure into the purchase. No matter what selling principles salesmen subscribe to, no matter how well they know their customers prior to their dealership visit, all of the salesmen's talent in evaluating and playing to the customers' means, needs and desires, must be orchestrated differently every time. There are an infinite number of recipes, but there is simply no cookbook.

Means, needs, and desires. Evaluating the customer's means, or capacity to afford a car, is called "qualifying the customer." That is, the salesman figures out which car, or in dealership parlance, "how much car," the customer can afford. Then there is need. The salesman really does care about the customer's driving habits because if the customer drives off in the wrong car, nobody wins: no customer satisfaction, no repeat business. Then there is desire, and exploiting desire is the key to making a profit, or "holding gross." When there is enthusiasm, there is fun, and often good profits for everybody, including the happy customer. But when there is indifference, the salesman must almost manually put the customer in a car and say, "Don't you love it?" The customer then replies, "Yes, as a matter of fact I do." After all, any person who visits a new car dealership and who doesn't at least like the potential purchase should either continue shopping until they do, or consider taking public transportation around town.

Surprisingly, most customers rarely have a realistic picture of their means, or "how much car" they can afford. Sometimes customers have not even thought through their driving needs. Customers often desire many different cars, giving the impression that they are confused, rather than simply undecided. That's why the salesman, who works on commission, and has little time to hear every customer's life story, must use quick tricks to determine what each customer can afford, needs, and as arrogant as it sounds, really wants. Many car salesmen are talented enough to do this in no time at all. Great customer analysis is one of the more difficult selling talents that separates great salesmen from the rest of the pack. They say, in the world of car dealerships, that every car is sold in the first hour, not during the price negotiation, so, while customers fear and focus on that later negative event, a good salesman knows the importance of the positive experience leading up to it.

During the moments before the sale kicks off, salesmen prepare, bracing themselves for the worst case scenario: the scared, defensive, doubting, weak customer. As they uncover key aspects of the customer's means, needs, desires, and intentions, salesmen must be able to switch approaches in a second. Customers often present a friendly face at first, only to panic or get exasperated a few minutes into their initial conversation with their salesmen. Why? Because, car dealerships are simply universally despised. No matter how people appear at first, they are, most of the time, wildly apprehensive. All good salesmen know this. One told me:

"I had a lady come in last Sunday, bought a car, a widow, alright, so she was very apprehensive about coming to a car dealership. She was there with her daughter, and I sensed her apprehension, because I am a salesman. I am a salesman, and I'm good at it, I'm damn good at what I do. So I said [to myself] you've got to be really cool with this. The key is that nobody wants to come to a... car store. Nobody. Nobody in their right mind wants to come to a car dealership. All the worst things happen. So it's my job to relax them and make a friend. 'Cause they've got to give a stranger twenty thousand dollars."

#3 HOW VALUABLE A CUSTOMER ARE YOU?

Some customers make appointments to come in, some have been referred, and some drive up with no established relationship to anyone at the dealership. Each of these customer types must be eased into a sale with a different orchestration of selling instruments: information, motivation, trust, and control.

When you visit a dealership, consider what your salesman might already know about *you* before you even arrive. Walk-ins or drive-ups are the most difficult. Salesmen have no prior knowledge about them, so it is like a blind date. There is no right place to start the conversation, and plenty of invisible traps waiting to kill the sale in its tracks.

Referrals are the best. A referral is the product of a customer who experienced a salesman's pitch and subsequent catch, actually lived to tell about it, *and* recommended that another human being have the same experience in the same salesman's hands. Referrals are tremendous ego boosters to even the most seasoned salesman. They afford the salesman the opportunity to act like a friend even before there are any grounds for friendship. Customers can't really see through the act, because for all they know the salesman and the referring customer may have bonded on a personal level. Car salesmen do have friends, and they do meet some through work. I have met two car salesmen who married their customers. In both cases, the customer bought the car from the salesmen, and both marriages lasted for many years.

An increasing number of dealerships hire services to field potential customer phone calls more efficiently. In the dealership where I worked, all phone calls that were identified by the switchboard as potential buyers' calls were transferred to somewhere near Chicago and handled by a professional appointment-making service. This service literally intercepts phone calls to dealerships so that professional phone agents can more effectively encourage callers to visit the dealership. They provide callers with answers to questions about current sales, car features, and even offer driving directions to the dealership. The customers then give their names and phone numbers to the call service professional in Illinois, who always calls himself or herself a certain name, such as Mr. Baker or Mrs. Baker. Then the professional faxes the information to the dealership. When the customers arrive at the dealership, they report that they have spoken with "Mr. Baker" or "Mrs. Baker." This is how the dealership knows that this person has called up and been primed, and that somewhere in a back office, there is a fax containing lots of information to help the salesman close the deal. Management then feeds the "Bakers," as these customers are called, to whichever salesmen they like, thus creating something for salesmen to fight about.

There is no way to convince you that salesmen have your every move pegged, except to tell about each element of your behavior they use to negotiate, when it comes time to negotiate.

#4 HOW SALESMEN WILL "HANDLE" YOU

"Just looking." When I sold cars, most of my customers told me that, as nonchalantly as they could. What customers say initially is much more driven by defense and fear than by straightforwardness. Sometimes shoppers do not have firm intentions, but most of the time they think they know what they want and *when* they want it. However, they want their salesman to be the last to know. They feel that withholding information is their most effective weapon. Salesmen then categorize buyers as either totally unfocused browsers, comparison shoppers, or price shoppers. In salesmen's minds, a different strategy is required to *nail* each one.

True Browsers are at the very beginning of the buying process. They know they need four doors and an engine, and they have resigned themselves to the unpleasant truth that they will spend a bundle. They drive around, gazing, glazing over, and overwhelming themselves with a lot of hoods and headlights, trying, usually unsuccessfully, to relax. Even if browsers learn nothing to bring them closer to a decision, that's OK, because the main goal is to avoid appearing too serious about buying. Browsers stroll across the showroom floor, that rough retail battlefield, and just because they are not suited up to fight, they think the opposing army isn't allowed to attack. So when the salesman tries to sell to them, they get flustered. Then they get angry. Salesmen feel that browsers must be finessed, that they can't be pressured in the least.

Comparison shoppers are like browsers in that they don't know exactly what they want to buy. But unlike browsers, comparison shoppers are on a mission, taking their medicine, actually stooping to talk to salesmen. But only for specific information. Comparison shoppers are heavily vested in being in control. What comparison shoppers want more than anything else is to test drive two or three cars in a class, then decide on one of those cars, based on the way they feel driving each car. Not on the salesman's jokes. Not on the number of cubic feet in the trunk. Not on the number of programmable radio stations. This is a rational approach to purchasing based on irrational feelings about the cars, and it's tough for the salesman to deal with. His mission is to get the buyer to buy into the fantasy of driving his new car home *today*, thereby keeping them from ever getting to the next dealership.

The **price shopper** is the most ferocious animal. The price shopper knows what he wants. Sure he loves his four-wheeled sweetheart, but he knows that the dealership on the other side of town can offer him the same joy for the same price, so he's going to back-burner his excitement, channel the capitalist spirit, and become a heavy negotiator, with the terrific tactics, calm and composure of the lawyer he watched on TV last night, with the intimidating air of the hit man the lawyer defended on TV last night, with the gusto, good looks, and heroic flair of all the heroes on all the TV he's ever seen. Tough guy for an afternoon. Who doesn't enjoy being justified in demanding a low price? The only problem with arriving at the dealership with a chip on your shoulder is that the salesman can see it when you walk in, and he will play that to his advantage, to be sure. Most buyers who have an "attitude" when they arrive at the dealership are not well-prepared in terms of knowing what they want, or even what they can afford. Generally, by the time they come into the dealership, price shoppers think they know what to expect, but part of the art of selling is adding more value to the car after the customer arrives. Salesmen normally don't do this well, though in theory it is the best way to sell anything. Customers who demand to buy cars they can't afford, hoping the price will drop unrealistically low just because they want it to are the rule, not the exception.

Many customers arrive at car dealerships with little or no understanding of the financial resources they require, or of their ability to ascertain financing. They don't have a grasp of what a credit company requires to lend them money to buy a car, how much taxes and insurance will run them, and so on. Salesmen need to get a sense of the customer's resources. Salesmen work on commission, and part of the reason for that is so that they will not waste their time going for futile joyrides in convertibles with teenagers who cannot afford any car at all, let alone a luxury vehicle. Salesmen are supposed to separate the serious buyers from the rest, and determine "how much car" each serious buyer can afford. That's called "qualifying the customer." Then the salesman is supposed to "land them on the car," the car that is at the top of their range of affordability.

Some customers stride into dealerships with confidence, announcing, "I am definitely going to buy a car today!" According to seasoned salesmen, these customers have no more probability of buying a car than customers who claim to be "just looking." Salesmen must ask follow-up questions to find out customers' shopping intentions and available means, and sometimes they do this by prying ever so gently into customers' private affairs. It's very hard to do because customers sense and resent it. A typical conversation between a browser and a salesman might go something like this:

- Salesman Says: Hi, I'm Joe Gargoyle. Welcome to Conrad Barker Motors. Can I help you today?
- Customer: Thanks, I'm just looking.
- *Salesman Thinks: He's looking at a black car. More people browse at sharp looking black cars than at any other color. More impulse buys are black cars.*
- Salesman Says: I see you are looking at this black car. Do you like black?
- Customer: Yeah.
- *Salesman Thinks: We are short on black cars, but have plenty of white cars in stock... Let's see what his resources are...*
- Salesman Says: Oh, I do too, I love black best, but my old car was black and it got too hot because I parked all day in the sun. I switched to white, which is great too. But black isn't a problem if you park inside all the time.
- Customer: Oh, that's no problem. I park in a garage at home and at work.
- *Salesman Thinks: Sounds like there's money. Lump sum or steady stream?*

• Salesman Says: No kidding. I wish this dealership had a garage for my car. It gets pretty hot here during the day. Where do you work?

• Customer: In the city, for years now.

• *Salesman Thinks: Cool, stability. Shirt says civil service. Major credit union.*

• Salesman Says: So you drive to work. I used to work in the city too. Which route do you take in?

• Customer: Parkway to the Roosevelt Bridge, takes twenty minutes.

• Salesman Says: Oh, so you live right around here?

• Customer: Little Falls.

• *Salesman Thinks: Little Falls? Wealth, got a good feeling here. Time to sell this guy the idea of owning THIS car by speaking in the future tense.*

• Salesman Says: Is this going to be your commuting car?

• Customer: Yes.

• *Salesman Thinks: Now compare this lovely new black car to whatever heap of crap the guy is driving today.*

• Salesman Says: What are you driving to work now?

• Customer: Well, actually, I am staying with my brother now, and using his car. I've had a little financial trouble lately, but it'll be cleared up pretty soon. I'm just waiting for the bank to...

• *Salesman Thinks: Credit problem. Abort mission, invent crisis, quick exit.*

Yes, that *is* how salesman think. They analyze everything a customer says.

WHAT YOUR SALESMAN IS DOING...

Now that you have some idea of what your salesman is look-ing for, you are ready to read about what your salesman will try to do to you during the sale. Remember that the point of this entire chapter is to show you that salesmen are constantly learning about you, and that there is nothing you can do about *that*. But here is some advance advice about what you *can* do: follow the Sixth Commandment (do not try to understand your salesman). Instead, follow the Fifth Commandment; write down everything your salesman says about the car and the deal. Period.

The following three sections are about what salesmen will try to establish: your **trust** in them, your **motivation** to buy, and their **control** over you.

#1 TRUST

Normal people hate the pressure of the car shopping expedi-tion. Salesmen try to get them to relax. They do this in a number of ways, but it always involves trust. Establishing trust with the cus-tomer is crucial in this pre-negotiation part of the sale, since *during* price negotiation whatever trust the salesman has established will be thrashed, almost to death, if the salesman is really talented. But how do salesmen get customers to trust them? Jimmy Jeffries gets people to like him:

"I nice 'em out. They like me whether they want to or not." But not all salesmen are likable buffoons like Jimmy. And then there is the gender problem, men and women trusting in different ways. Philippe Seguin explains how he lets women trust him, and helps men trust themselves:

Women customers are a lot easier to deal with. Not

in the sense that they're not as good shoppers, but if you give them the feeling of confidence, then you can do what you want, because then they'll trust you. The key is to get the customer's trust. If you don't get the customer's trust, it's an ongoing battle, and that's very important, because usually they're going to refer customers to you if you've treated them well. So the idea is, if you're nice the first day, and you're not nice the rest of the time, it's a losing proposition. You basically have to be like a duck, where water just rolls over you. How to turn the worst of situations to your benefit: Stop blaming the other guys. 'Yes sir, you had a bad car. It's an unfortunate situation. But let's make that a better situation. Why don't you trade the car and get the misery over.' 'Yeah, makes sense.' Always get the guy to go, 'Yeah...yeah...' and psychologically, he's convincing himself.

Salesman Hugo Hevesy describes how the most effective way to get people to relax is to have fun, and how most Americans miss the fun in the transaction. Hugo always has fun, no matter what.

"See, the sad part of it is, most people when they get into this sort of thing, and try to get resolutions, actually they almost deal with it as a war. But what I try to do, if I'm in a good mood, and I'm awake, and I got enough sleep, and all those other things are in place, is that I always try to add that personal touch, the single most important thing. So, I always try to have a personal relationship with the person I'm dealing with, and almost value that more than the problem we are dealing with, and I show that to people. And people appreciate that. And they loosen up to it. I care about them, I'm playing with them, I'm enjoying myself, they're having fun. Even though it might be a difficult thing, that you know, we are talking about big numbers and they have to work very hard for that money."

#2 MOTIVATION

Salesmen need to "build value" in the product in order to sell it. No matter what, customers won't feel as though they have gotten a good deal unless they are really excited about the car, and since cars are so expensive, the more benefits customers appreciates, the easier it is to part with their money.

Who has ever really stopped to methodically examine the parts of a car? We all think we know enough to choose a car, but when we get to the dealership, all of a sudden the salesman starts talking about the suspension technology, the evolution of the braking system, an infinite list of car features. As the customers hear about these features, they admit that they are all very important, and they become filled with tension: should they spend time thinking about all of this, their minds awash with the salesman's tidal wave of car details, or do they rush through the sale in an attempt to avoid relinquishing control to the salesman? It depends on the salesman, and it depends on the customer.

The show-and-tell portion of the car sale is called the "walkaround" or "six position," or "five point," and it is an art form. Theoretically, the salesman stands at five or six different points around the car, enumerating and describing the benefits of each feature. The walkaround is a serious event. There are competitions for best walkaround at salesmen's conventions. Winners fly to Hawaii or receive five figure checks. Car manufacturers support events that motivate salesmen to excel at the walkaround. It's really the only presentation device the salesman has to show off the product in any reliable and meaningful way. Almost all of the product knowledge the salesman learns in training is conveyed during the walkaround. Any product information not presented in the walkaround is not guaranteed to ever reach the customer.

Jimmy Jeffries, the training manager where I worked, taught a simple selling method: point to a product feature, list the feature's benefits, over and over and over again. Although anybody can tell a customer that it is best to have breakaway mirrors, those that bend back against the car when smacked, breakaway mirrors are better off demonstrated than explained. So, when customers least expect it, a good salesman smacks the mirrors hard, bounces on the bumper, crawls into the trunk, through the car, and out the driver's door, especially if there are children to impress. Jimmy Jeffries told us to point to a feature and list its benefits, but there are a million ways to point, and a million ways to communicate that a feature has benefits, which makes the walkaround performance art.

Sometimes salesmen are successful for the very reasons they should be failures. James Lind, Saab salesman, taught me that one day as I was pretending to shop for a car (but really doing research for this book). From the moment I walked in, the lone salesman didn't seem to want me in his showroom. After about three minutes, which is an eternity to be left alone in a car dealership, he asked me what I was looking for. He didn't ask me if I wanted a test drive. Nor was he forthcoming with information. I had to ask if it would be alright for me to drive a car. His indifference and unresponsiveness would have gotten him fired on the spot at my dealership.

James was not enthusiastic about selling, though I did not rule out the possibility that he was enthusiastic about cars. James and I got into the car, and since it was a cold winter day, we sat there for ten minutes as the engine warmed up. While we sat, James pointed, switched and turned knobs, explaining absolutely all of the interior features, and their precise impact on the car's performance. It was then that James Lind started to make sense to me, because it was then that I learned that he had spent years and years working in Saab Parts, not Saab Sales. He's a Saab man, not just some salesman who drifts from dealership to dealership.

James knew Saab products best not from their reputation or advertising, and not from their service reliability record, but from the point of view of their parts. He knew their design and history cold. He even told me anecdotes about Saab's Swedish designers. He explained to me how Saab's engineers had adapted much of their cars' instrumentation designs from aircraft cockpit design. For instance, the dashboard buttons are differentiated by not only the labels on them, but also by texture and by shape, to be operable in the dark or when the driver is watching the road. There was a very interesting feature called "black panel," in which all of the displays go black except for the speedometer- great for night driving. Before we even left the parking lot, James Lind, the out-of-place, awkward salesman, had practically sold me a car based on the thoughtfulness of its dashboard design, and I was only pretending to shop!

#3 CONTROL

Controlling the customer and controlling the sale are the rules of the game. In the car business, that means salesmen *lead* customers, which translates to salesmen needing to be happier and more confident, and therefore more enthusiastic, than their customers. Of course each salesman has to be fully confident that *this* customer could do nothing better than to buy *this* car. Easier said than done. In fact, communicating that certainty and enthusiasm is the most challenging part of selling. When done successfully, customers just try to keep up, never sensing that their single-minded goal of being as enthusiastic as the salesman is controlling them. But once customers sense even this indirect control over them, the sale is over; it just won't happen.

In the high end, customers have more money and are used to controlling many more elements of their lives, so the control game is even more difficult. A high-end salesman on "controlling the customer":

> In a volume cycle business, it's possible. In the high end, it's not possible, because you have to give the customer the impression that he's controlling. That's what they like to see. You go along like, 'Yes Mr. Customer, of course Mr. Customer, no problem Mr. Customer.' And all along, you're psychologically controlling the customer to the point that you make him say what you want.
>
> In the high end situation, usually you're going to pre-order cars based on the salesman's capacity. So, you want to pick what you have coming in, and not what he wants. Let's assume I have four black cars coming. The first thing you do is you ask, 'Hey, what color is your present car, Mr. Customer?' And the guy says, 'I drive a white car.' And you say [to yourself], Ooh, white car, complete opposite of black! Then you move on to the next step. The idea is if the guy says, 'Yeah, I have a white car, but you know it's got such and such a drawback,' then you emphasize the drawback, and then you carry on, on another topic, talk about the features of the car. Then, when he least expects it, like when he's *gazing,* you say, 'You know, this car is most *awesome* in black...' Then he's starting to think about black. The pressure tactic in the high end is a road right to disaster.

Conrad Barker Motors sold about three hundred new cars per month and kept a huge inventory, usually about five hundred cars. The idea was for customers to arrive, buy, and be able to drive home the cars they bought, all in the same day. That's all part of the volume mentality: get 'em *into* the car, then *off* the lot, *in* the car. Problem was, there were no numbered parking spaces for the five hundred-plus car inventory. If the customer wanted a specific car and there was only one exactly like it, the salesman had to run around and search through five hundred cars in three parking garages in order to find it, and often it was parked in by another car, which required an extra trip back to the dealership building for the blocking car's key. While this hunt went on, the customer stood outside on the blacktop, getting hot and frustrated. I complained about the sorry state of inventory management, but a salesman explained to me that making customers wait was part of the control game; slow 'em down and wear 'em down to the point that they can't imagine going through the whole ordeal again at another dealership.

THE TEST DRIVE

The test drive is an extremely important part of the sale because during the test drive customers feel ownership of the car. They place themselves in a narrative, imagine a story in which they get to drive the car home. It is also during the test drive that the salesman has the opportunity to motivate the buyer further, and to play countless tricks to foster trust in him.

All kinds of things happen during the test drive. Simple tactile experiences evoke emotional sensations that are more powerful, lasting, and greater than any imagined fantasy about having the car.

Whether a sufficient dose of magic is delivered by the salesman, the new car smell, or the feeling of the engine idling, the magic happens. Some time after the customer gets behind the wheel, he becomes king, he *owns* the car, at least right there, right then. This transition requires the salesman's graceful reversion from role of "master of automotive technology," back to role of schmuck. Jimmy Jeffries practiced this art form with expertise worthy of ten

Academy Awards. His device was humor mixed with self-efface-ment, and he did it like this: He'd drive customers to a beautiful, gated mansion, then say he lived there, and had to go in because he forgot his wallet that morning. He'd stop the car, open the door, and start to get out. Mrs. Customer is impressed, and at the perfect instant, he turns around and smiles, and admits that he is only jok-ing. By confessing that he is not insanely wealthy *and* that he is a liar, but only for fun, he fosters the customer's trust.

Jimmy's car sales academy test drive lesson included a drive through picturesque countryside, past grazing horses and huge trees in rocky, overgrown fields. Jimmy screeched-stopped the minivan full of stunned salesmen-in-training. He pointed down a lushly landscaped private drive to a stunning home, set in the middle of a full acre of perfectly groomed lawn. Parked in the driveway outside the house were two small cars, the very cars we were learn-ing to sell. Jimmy said that he often stopped there during the test drive, each time pretending to notice those two cars for the very first time. "Just look at who buys our cars! These people can afford more expensive cars, but they obviously are smart with money, and they know what a good value our cars are." There are many clever test drive devices. Salesmen are always trying to destabilize their customers, to keep control of the sale. Don't let them. Stay focused on the car and the sale, and write down everything they say.

FIFTH COMMANDMENT - TO DO

Buy a notebook. Start writing down anything you learn about the car you want to buy, and where you read it or heard it. Put your list of dealerships in this notebook. Keep your notebook handy- it's your friend!

Chapter Six

SIXTH COMMANDMENT: DO NOT TRY TO "UNDERSTAND" YOUR CAR SALESMAN

Do not try to "understand" your car salesman. You won't. Car salesmen are very creative. To succeed at sales, salesmen must be natural psychologists. They will probably understand you better than you will ever understand them. You cannot guess what they will do next; trying will only distract you from the sale.

The Sixth Commandment and the Fifth Commandment (write down everything your salesman says,) work together; focus on the car and the deal, and do *not* focus on the guy trying to *sell* you the car and *make* the deal. Why do I dedicate a whole chapter to something you should not do? Because, salesmen are constantly trying to "make friends" with you. The best way to avoid this trap, and it is a trap, is to invest zero effort in trying to understand your salesman. Sounds brutal, but it's true.

Chapter Six tells you who becomes car salesmen, why, what they are taught, and what they think they are doing. The moral of these stories is that car salesmen's minds are scary places and you should not *want* to share, understand, or even entertain their versions of reality. There are, of course, exceptions. But if your salesman is so exceptional and you want him to become your best friend, make friends **after** you make a deal on the car. No matter how friendly and nice your salesman is, *stay focused on the car and the deal.* Like the last chapter, the information in the rest of this chapter is meant to scare you into staying focused on your car and your deal, *not* on your salesman.

THE CAR DEALERSHIP DILEMMA

We Americans love to hate our car salesmen. Salesmen are saddled with the notoriety of the entire car retailing industry because they are the industry's only representatives who deal directly with the public. But hold on: just as car salesmen are known as the bad boys of retail, car shoppers are the bad boys and girls of the consumer realm. In other words, car salesmen hate their customers just as much as car buyers hate their salesmen.

Car salesmen think, quite rightly, that car buyers are conflicted, that they are driven simultaneously by their love of shopping, their love of cars, and their hatred of spending money. These conflicting feelings produce a state of confusion and indecision, and so the salesman, who more than anything else wants to avoid wasting his own time, because he works on commission, tries to sort out the buyer's conflict as quickly as possible, while not exactly wearing kid gloves. That is, in a nutshell, the car salesman's job. Not very appealing, huh?

To car salesmen, car buyers are nothing more than a checkbook, a pen, a driver's license, and a pair of feet in need of a clutch and a gas pedal, all stuffed into one pair of jeans. To car buyers, car salesmen are walking, talking, dishonest advertisements. Who is right? Who is better? Is there any way to transcend these shallow views?

Yes, there is. Admit that a car dealership is a marketplace, and that a negotiation is a battle of sorts, so that each side views the other side as "in the wrong" when things do not go well. In other words, just ignore the dilemma, it cannot be avoided, and it is not personal. There are good people and bad people on both sides of the bargaining table. The point of telling you all about who becomes salesmen, why, what they are taught and how they think is to convince you that these are strange and cunning people, and that you will do best to ignore everything about them except for what they tell you about the car you want to buy.

WHO BECOMES A CAR SALESMAN?

Jimmy Jeffries hires, trains, and supervises rookie salesmen at Conrad Barker Motors. After having hired close to a hundred and fifty salesmen per year for over five years, he knows who will stick. Jimmy rarely hires women because he thinks they can't sell cars in a high-pressure environment. He says women can't package and sell the car fantasy the way men can, and he should know because he is a top car salesman and a top recruiter of car salesmen. But Jimmy also used to make a living recruiting women to sell fantasy, only without the car attached. Twenty years ago, Jimmy Jeffries hired teams of saleswomen for the job of prostitute in the most successful "fantasies only" prostitution business in Washington, DC.

At seventeen years old, Jimmy Jeffries dropped out of high school to tour the country with a stripper, playing bass guitar in her backup band. Thirty-three years later, he had been married and beyond four times to a go-go dancer, two bartenders and a hairdresser. He had surfed cycles of success as the owner of blues bars, go-go bars, restaurants, a "fantasies-only" escort service, and finally as a car salesman and manager.

What all of these businesses have in common is the coordination of a group of people who work together, and, if nothing else, Jimmy Jeffries knows how to pick teams, train them, and then send them out to work. He told me once that he never hired experienced car salesmen or bartenders because, "if they are going to make mistakes, they might as well be my mistakes."

Here is a guy who has mastered the interviewing and "training" of women to sell sexual fantasy to very wealthy men, and the interviewing and training of men to sell the car fantasy to American men and women. Jimmy's training in the psychological trenches of human nature, in the bars and go-go clubs of America may seem seedy, but it's the Ivy League for the study of human behavior, and finishing school for how to take advantage of human frailties, fantasies, and plain old hope. Ninety-nine out of a hundred people walking into his dealership off the street are no match for Jimmy Jeffries.

Car salesmen occupy a common state of mind once they are heaped together on the showroom floor. But they find their way into the business from various states of nature, states of disgrace, and states of political turmoil. I met many car salesmen during and after the time I worked in dealerships. Some of them were boring people who had nothing to say to me or to anybody else. But a great diversity of car salesmen, particularly the more successful ones, were terribly compelling.

Selling cars is a very creative endeavor. Every customer is different and every customer has different thoughts. An appreciation for different values is essential if a person is going to spend every day trying to understand and sway different customers to make what is, in the end, a very simple transaction: money in exchange for a car. Hugo Hevesy spent his first nineteen years behind the iron curtain, in an increasingly intense effort to leave, systematically overcoming all of the Hungarian government's objections to his departure. Once it was behind him, this experience gave Hugo an appreciation for the unsettled life, creativity, and freedom of choice.

"It took a long time. After I finished high school, it took me a year and a half, two years to get my passport. It's extremely difficult for a young person, because you have to serve at least two years in the army. Being a little bit smart, I realized I gotta do something.

You can do two things. You can run and get shot at, or you try to get a passport, one way or another when they let you leave, thinking that you're coming back... They had two different kinds of passports. One passport was for the Eastern Bloc and one was for the West. And of course the eastern passport was easy. I used to have one at the age of fourteen.

"I had to get a little bit smarter to get a western passport and I was working on it for two years. You had to get permission from every sort of organization and things like that and you have to figure out what kind of things they want to hear. You just tell them what they want to hear or you do favors or you make the right moves and they say yes. It's like a Kafka kind of nightmare. That's how it is. You go and you fill out the forms and you wait in line and you hope for the best and if it doesn't- they throw it back on you and you try to figure out why, where to go next. You know, it's just how it works. And it works, in a sense. It's just extremely time consuming and it totally wears people down and kills them. First I told them I was going to Austria, to a soccer game. You see the way it works... they are not very consistent. It's very difficult to run any country in a very consistent manner, to not leave any loopholes."

Hugo Hevesy is unbelievably patient. He had to be to have survived and make it to America, to learn English, and to be hungry enough to compete and succeed selling cars. If you think you have half as much determination as Hugo Hevesy, you are already exceptional.

Other salesman took different paths. A brief history of Henry Washington, in his own words:

Before the car business? I grew up in New York. I was in school, ROTC. Reserve Officer. Went to Viet Nam. Got commissioned, served two tours in Viet Nam, war hero, combat helicopter pilot, flew two hundred and seventy-three combat missions. I extended my tour. I loved it. I was twenty-one. I'm still in it. I still fly. Since then, man, I've done a whole lot of things. I worked at a major clothing manufacturer. I joined them as an accountant. I hated accounting. My degree's in accounting. From there, I got into sales. I sold shirts for a long time... I went into government... at Grade Fourteen, Step Six. That's like, all the way up there. I was writing the city's overall economic development policy. My MBA is in finance and entrepreneurial development. I went to government for a while, wrote a whole lot of stuff, had a lot of fun down there.

More ventures followed: import-export, janitorial supply, computers; always in sales...

I was doing a consulting project for a group of lawyers. They tried to beat me. They paid me half, wanted to get out of the rest. So, in putting the deal together, a guy and I became friends. Eighteen months, we did 5.7 million dollars, and then he stole, he admitted he stole half a million dollars out of the company. Yeah, he admitted that. Only reason why I'm not in jail is 'cause I couldn't get my hands on a pistol. Took off for two months after that, and knew people in the car business and decided to try it. Never really liked it, but I was good at it 'cause I know *people*.

This entrepreneur, fighter pilot, chemical, and shirt salesman, broke down after a bad deal. Disillusioned, cynical, and with no other ambition, he tumbled into a profession in which he could fly psychological missions into enemy territory, and strategically work his numbers into customers' minds. It is difficult to imagine a scarier opponent in a car sales negotiation than a fighter pilot-accountant with decades' experience in sales. If you think your car salesman is a simpleton, he is probably working his magic on you. Stay focused on the sale, not on him.

HOW DEALERSHIPS HIRE

Sam Schroeder, owner of a small dealership:

> How we should hire... or how we hire? The industry traditionally has hired by seat of the pants. They like somebody's facial expression, voice inflection, toenails, they have the job. And if it didn't work out, car salesmen were very easy to fire. Increasingly what has happened is there are a number of companies that have actually been testing for new car salespeople and service people. The National Auto Dealers Association has a very rigorous program of hiring practices and training and testing. The reality is that only about ten percent of dealers use it. Most dealers still hire by gut feel. They don't hire people with formal educations, or if they do, they get nervous, because most dealer principals have very little education... That is changing, but until probably about ten years ago there was high suspicion amongst car dealers of hiring education.

Questioned about a brand new salesman in his dealership, Sam Schroeder explained how he was hired:

> Yeah, Daniel Chase. He came from another dealership, had reasonably good training, a guy that's interest-

ed in gross profit. We called ten customers- all salesmen keep customer records. We asked him for his records. I called ten of the customers and said, "Do you know this guy?" Now, if they didn't know this guy, then I didn't want to know him because I think you should remember your car salesman. It's the second most important purchase you have in your life after your house. Positive feedback on eight of them. One of them said that she didn't want to deal with him because he asked her out, and another said, 'He was a great salesman but he wanted a bottle of wine from me.' Then he went through a rigorous interview process with myself, and my sales manager. And in my dealership it is a practice to have someone in my service or parts department to interview him. After we interviewed him, like we interview everyone, the three of us sat together and analyzed his talents, called up some of his references, and offered him a job.

One year later, Daniel Chase fled his job at Sam's dealership, leaving behind him a two thousand dollar debt to star salesman Bruno the Shark, so nicknamed for his habit of continuously circling the car as he demonstrates its features to his customers. Chase also left behind a foiled posse of law enforcement officials who were in hot pursuit of him for reasons unrelated to his car-selling career. Three months after Chase disappeared, he called Sam's dealership to request that they send along his back pay. The dealership accountant asked where she could send the money, she recorded the address Chase gave her, and then she called the police. The police apprehended Chase, proving that it doesn't take brains to be a successful car salesman. It just takes a lot of nerve, and so far, no company has figured out a way to do a background check on that.

WHO DEALERSHIPS HIRE

Who in the world would choose to be a car salesman? There is no average candidate for the job. It is a profession of exceptions, but somehow Jimmy Jeffries can pick 'em out.

"You know one trait I have, I'm a people person. I can look at a person and interview a person, talk to 'em for five minutes, and pretty well put 'em together. That's why I've been the most successful training manager they've had."

We were five students on the first day of training. I can't say that anybody in my car sales training class struck me as proud to be learning how to sell cars. It seemed as though everybody there either threw themselves into a last, desperate hope for success, or were pulled in by a perhaps misguided sense of adventure (certainly the case for me). The only thing we seemed to have in common was that we were there.

My favorite classmate was a very striking, very big, very black, young bald man. Since leaving his native Ethiopia several years ago, Menelik had worked in the restaurant business all over the United States. Through his then current job of publicizing parties and other restaurant events in Washington, DC, Menelik had met thousands of people. His vision was to sell used cars through his public relations clientele. I liked Menelik for two reasons: his goals were realistic, and he was scary as hell when he got mad. He never boiled over, he simmered.

Menelik's Ethiopian friend was a guy named Earl. At the time Menelik applied for his job, Earl was Assistant Manager of Used Car Sales. Earl had recommended to the management that Menelik be hired, and though Jimmy Jeffries hired Menelik to sell used cars, he thought Menelik needed at least some new car sales training. Menelik would work in Used Car Sales, but was resigned to going through the New Car Sales training with the rest of us.

Before Menelik's first day of training, Earl threw a wrench in Menelik's plans. Earl went missing from work, which greatly diminished the weight given to the character endorsement he lent Menelik. Earl was gone, simply disappeared, leaving only his Mercedes in the parking lot. As the sun rose and set on Conrad Barker Motors, dealership personnel started to worry about Earl. I was spooked. Environments in which people routinely disappeared for longer than say, a day, were not something I wanted to get used to. But in this world, such a mystery seemed to be unusual though not unheard of. Secretly, I suspected that Earl had been involved in foul play, and that the dealership boys were not keen to start a formal search for fear of what they might turn up.

After one week, Earl showed up. Just walked in one day. He had been partying, that's all. Earl was fired, which meant that Menelik no longer had a friend in management, and was reduced to just another thug in car sales training. But Jeffries regarded Menelik as a smart pillar of strength and cunning. With the salesman dropout rate as high as it is, and it's high, Jimmy took Earl's elimination as an opportunity to reassign Menelik to New Car sales. When Jimmy told Menelik he'd be selling new cars, Menelik's face fell a thousand feet, but he didn't complain and he didn't quit. He just rolled with the punches for several months until Earl resurfaced in another used car dealership. Soon after that, the two compatriots were reunited and sold used cars happily ever after. Menelik was a survivor from day one.

I don't remember the second student's name. Jimmy referred to him only as "The Bouncer" because he was short and dense and wore a scowl. He didn't seem to be too smart, as he kept missing the "finish the sentence" quizzes, short and dense in intellect too. The bouncer never showed up for day two.

Student number three was Miles. During the entire first week of car sales training, I wondered why Jimmy had hired Miles. Miles was not slick, not graceful, not a talker. Miles was nothing to look at. One day, right in front of him, Jimmy remarked on Miles' crazy smile and bewildered stare. Jimmy said it was effective and might freak people out; more or less *scare* them into buying a car. Mesmerized into dropping twenty grand? Interesting hypothesis. I see his point; sort of the anti-authority figure, whose rooted insanity and compulsion belies his apparently meek disposition. I thought Jimmy must really be insightful, desperate, or bored with regular people, to hire a guy like that. Then again, regular people don't apply to be car salesmen.

Like everyone else, Miles had a story. After serving in the Navy, Miles had taught English in Japan for thirteen years. At least once a day he told me that he was learning to sell cars because he had nothing better to do with his life, and since nobody was relying on him for support since his wife left him, why not try something different? I never got over wanting to cry every time he said it. Miles had a rosy complexion and looked innocent and meek. He combed his hair compulsively, which was funny because his short-sleeved dress shirts were as wrinkled as used aluminum foil. But Miles betrayed his innocent air by divulging surprisingly detailed knowledge of Japanese drug trafficking and criminal justice issues. Miles seemed listless and lost, not the kind of guy who would jump out of bed each morning to haggle with anybody about anything. Sure enough, Miles lasted about a week on the floor before a more seasoned salesman stole his customer. I saw him leaving on what turned out to be his last day, almost in tears.

Hector was a Cuban-American medical surgical technician of some kind. He struck me as exceedingly unmotivated. Hector wasn't just unmotivated, he was lazy, and he was a complainer. To make him unbearably annoying, Hector had a root canal during the first week of training, so he slurred his speech, which made him seem even lazier. One day my whole class went across the street to get a burger for lunch. While we ate, Hector announced that he was going to meet with eight doctors later that day. Then he stopped chewing and looked around the table, gauging our reactions. Nobody seemed to notice or care. Should we have asked why he was going to meet with eight doctors? Nobody did. Nobody cared. I wondered if Hector felt imprisoned in our training class, eager to break into a new career even before his first day as a car salesman. Through the rest of his burger, Hector slurred and mumbled doubts, as though in a car dealership confessional. He just wasn't ready for the long hours, working weekends and holidays... He knew his fiancée could not make the decision for him, so he would have to make it... Already, he didn't like the pressure. Hector muttered these doom and gloom bouquets in between bites of juicy wet burger drowning in ketchup, relish, and salsa. The condiments on his burger mixed together and oozed slowly out from inside the bun, which was clutched between his tense hands. Like Hector's slushy ambition, desire and discipline, the red-green mush dribbled to a swamp on his plate until he abandoned it to the trash and dawdled back to training class. Like Miles, Hector never embraced the challenge. One day a pungent breeze blew him down the dusty divided suburban highway and we never saw him again.

Late in the first week of training, looking young, hip, and together, enter Winston. Winston was excitement, Winston was enthusiasm, and Winston knew someone high up in the company, which is why he was allowed to start training late. A couple of days later we were asked to photocopy our drivers' licenses, and that is when we learned that Winston's driving license had been suspended. Winston would never be a car salesman. Did he think he could sell cars without a valid driver's license? I was shocked, looked to Jimmy for a reaction, but Jimmy Jeffries just sat still and shook his head from side to side to side, and closed his eyes.

The day Winston left the dealership via public transportation,

Gordon the Nordstrom shoe salesman joined our class. Gordon insisted on attending Jimmy's informal, un-air-conditioned car sales training classes in a formal Nordstrom suit. Gordon made it through training despite his vast arrogance and refusal to "play" with the rest of us. He did poorly at negotiation role-playing because he had no sense of humor and inevitably insulted his role-playing customers. I was partially responsible for his emotional downfall since I took it upon myself to bring him to the point of exasperation as he played the salesman to my role of angry customer. I was determined to have fun, and I did. Gordon never had fun, which told me that Gordon would not last long in the business. It was too dirty for him. He was used to kneeling down before women, putting their little stockinged feet into shoes and earnestly asking, "How does that feel in the instep, ma'am?" He was totally out of his element. Once Gordon demonstrated his total lack of sales initiative, Jimmy started to remark, "you can't be a clerk, you gotta be a salesman, gentlemen." After we graduated from training, Gordon sat at his desk in the showroom for one slow, twelve-hour day, and then he disappeared, to where, nobody knows, but our money was on nine to five nirvana.

Starting with a total of fifteen to thirty applicants, Jimmy Jeffries accepted seven trainees. Of those seven, five "graduated" from J.J.'s training academy. Of those five, only two (including me, and I was only hanging on in the interest of research,) lasted a month or longer on the sales floor.

Excluding myself, only Menelik the Ethiopian prevailed, not only through training class and one month on the floor, but through month after month in the business. My other five classmates were all-American types, more or less, and they all failed miserably. This outcome is not exceptional. The rosy, balding, fifty-something American car salesman in the checked sport coat and stained tie is an endangered stereotype. Sure, there are plenty living out their days in dealerships, but they're the veterans. The new breed is young, slick, and the successful ones among them are almost never white, American men.

A map of the world is pinned to the wall in a manager's office at Conrad Barker Motors. This map seems out of place since everything else in the room reflects the insular cultural world of car dealerships. Yet, this map is not idle decoration, nor is it a sarcastic put-on. Seventeen countries on five continents are dotted with shiny red map pins: El Salvador, Ecuador, Peru, Chile, Argentina, Senegal, Morocco, Egypt, Ethiopia, Hungary, Turkey, Russia, Afghanistan, Singapore, China, Canada, and the United States. These countries represent the dealership salesmen's countries of origin. Conrad Barker, United Nations of salesmanship, employs people from many places and many lives. They dream about going to America to make big money selling the American dream, the automobile. Car-cultural ambassador Conrad Barker teaches people how to sell cars to Americans, though it seems that American salesmen are generally too deeply immersed in the dream to sell it to themselves.

HOW DEALERSHIPS TRAIN CAR SALESMEN

Asked, by me, if he has a philosophy of car sales training, Jimmy Jeffries had this to say:

> My philosophy is you need to come to work and sell cars. I don't give a shit if the managers are in a bad mood, everybody's in a bad mood, if the world around you is crumbling. You come to work with one purpose only: to sell a car. If you come to work with that one purpose only, to sell a car, get your name on the board, by the end of the month, you'll have twenty plus cars, and

you'll have a five thousand dollar paycheck. If you don't come to work with that in your mind, and you don't hold that every day, you're not going to sell crap.

I asked Jimmy what he meant by that.

It means I had better have my ass there from nine to nine, I had better sell a car. It's the only job in the world where you don't need any education... What do you need education for? People buy cars from people they like. If they like you, they're gonna buy the car. What do they care if you have a master's degree, or a degree in this, or...

I reminded Jimmy that a salesman needs to know the features of the car.

"Just common sense." I asked if that was everything a salesman needed to know.

"Yeah, the features, and what else? What did I train you? Features and what else? Already you forgot. The most important thing." The competition, I suggested.

"No no. The most important thing. You tell the features and what's the most important thing after the features?" The benefits, I guessed out loud.

"Yeah, exactly. That's the most important thing... That's how you hold gross. That's how you make money." I suggested that knowing the benefits of a car is just common sense, that anybody could figure out the benefits of a car.

"Well if they can't, they're in serious trouble. They can't hold a job even in McDonald's. That's, you know, that's my philosophy in life."

Jimmy Jeffries describes his car sales training curriculum:

Well, first of all there is always a week of product knowledge, 'cause I move it slow. Then we do the selling process. You go out and write the cars [the paperwork]. When you take people and put 'em in two weeks, they get more comfortable with the dealership, they meet a few people, so that when they get on the floor they're a lot more relaxed... Five days, then put 'em out on the floor, they're scared; they're not going to come to work. But the survival rate is a lot better when you give two weeks. They're familiar with the dealership, they're standing around, at home.

Ninety percent of the two weeks I spent at Conrad Barker Motors' salesman training consisted of learning to instill intimidation and relaxation in customers, simultaneously. Instilling intimidation and relaxation also makes up ninety percent of the acculturation necessary for survival in a car dealership. Most of the "lessons" Jimmy "taught" were his car showroom war stories. Jimmy has a fantastic ability to talk about himself and his success as a salesman, but almost no ability to train anybody else, yet train them he does. Several times per day, Jimmy would sing his training refrain: "Cars and bars, same culture."

One of Jimmy's training techniques was discouragement. He used discouragement to train and to test. He discouraged through intimidation, telling tales of abuse and burnout while simultaneously boring us nearly to death with car and driving theory. Then he'd rouse us back from a comatose state with live-action absurdity. Jimmy's training course was an up-close view of and into himself, a successful car salesman. To many, "successful car salesman" is an oxymoron, a depressing prospect. But more than the concept of Jimmy, it was the prolonged and intense exposure to Jimmy that was at least half the test. Could we stand to be around J.J. and others like him? For most, the answer is no.

Once Jimmy has finished training the class, the graduates hit the sales floor, and it is Jimmy's responsibility to see that the more experienced salesmen and managers don't eat the rookies for breakfast:

> My worst enemies in the car business are the sales managers and the general manager. Why? Because you've got two separate things here. Their team is only focused on one thing: selling cars and holding gross. They don't want to be bothered training and working with rookies. So, my job is to try to work with them and protect them as much as possible. So when I take a rookie and put him down on the floor, and we're under fire, you think they're going to be concerned because you're new? They don't give a shit that you're new. You get out of the way; we're there to sell cars. So my job is to try to balance the two, and keep the rookies.

> Look, hang in there man, get past this crap,' like I told you in training. You know you've got to take some shit, there's a lot of shit involved, but when people get down there and they realize how much shit is involved, they can't cut it. They go, 'Ooh, I can't do it.' And there's guys that go down there and hit it right off the bat. Rudy. Fouad. Guys that have no previous sales experience. But one thing I notice about a lot of guys, Hugo Hevesy, Rudy, is they have a certain underlying thing, an ego thing, that you need to stroke, and when you stroke that you get more production out of it.

Of course, it's all a matter of perspective. The more successful salesmen think they learned everything on their own, and that if anybody seems to have helped them, taught them, or was otherwise kind to them, it is merely coincidental to their success. Hugo Hevesy:

"Jimmy Jeffries hires the people, he trains them, and then they normally quit." Hugo Hevesy calls Jimmy's training course "the biggest laugh on earth. It's... I'm shocked. I think that people are responsible mainly for their own actions. So you can't blame the guy who tells them the tale, Jeffries, you know."

Jimmy Jeffries has little more complimentary to say about Hugo Hevesy:

"The trouble with Hugo is, his perception of what's really going on is so far away... that he is the salesman we constantly have to bring down, put down to earth, 'cause he gets lost."

Car salesmen are experts at explaining the universe. They wrap up every detail that might bother you, make it all consistent, perfect, no problem. That is why it is so amusing to hear them peg each other down to the last detail, to explain away all differences and diversity among them as (the other person's) character flaw. Not only do they survive by recognizing, encouraging, and profiting from customers' car fantasies, they also keep themselves above conflict amongst themselves by explaining away all other points of view. Car salesmen don't only sell cars. They also sell their own lives and minds, every minute of every day, to their customers, to their colleagues, and especially to themselves. Good car salesmen make everything upbeat, right, and whole, in their minds, in their hearts, and all around them. Learning to convey that is learning to sell fantasy.

SIXTH COMMANDMENT - TO DO

DO NOTHING. Do not try to understand what makes your car salesman tick. It does not matter and it will only distract you from getting the best deal you can get.

Chapter Seven

SEVENTH COMMANDMENT: DO NOT LIE

"All customers are liars." Wait!! Jimmy Jeffries was about to train five innocent citizens to sell cars, and this is how he chose to begin their education! Why so negative? Why so adversarial? Everybody knows that salesmen are the liars and customers are the victims. Sure, the power of desire and fantasy shapes car buyers' perceptions of affordability. Sure, salesmen withhold information on the car lot in an attempt to guard themselves from aggressive sales pitches. But in the end, who is being cagey, salesmanlike, aggressive, evasive, and who just plain lies? The expected news is that salesmen are professional fantasy sellers and fantasy implies built-in deception. The bad news is that at car dealerships, everybody lies, including the customers.

Car buyers are not professional negotiators, and when the drama of car sales in America eventually results in a price negotiation of some kind, customers become overwhelmed and often lie first, lie unconvincingly, and only hurt themselves in the process. Worst of all, they make the car salesman's mantra true: All customers *are* liars. Of course, customers never intend to lie, but neither do salesmen. It's just that the structure of the price negotiation makes it almost impossible not to. So, how much lying really goes on? Between the salesman's lies and the customer's lies, a lot, but salesmen don't always lie more than customers. Salesmen just lie better than customers, which is why they are perceived as the ones who are doing the ripping off... and once the lying begins, salesmen usually win bigger than if the lying never started.

Stay anchored in the truth when you negotiate. You will have more self-confidence and be more difficult to outsmart.

Here is what will happen to you if you lie to your car salesman: He will catch on immediately. He deals with liars all day long and he is expert at detecting lies *and* telling lies. He will lie back to you. He is probably a better liar than you are anyway. But if he isn't, the sales manager is. And if *he* isn't, you can be sure the general manager is. If you have a trick, they have probably seen it and know five ways around it. You will be on their turf. You have less information than they have. They will outnumber you. They will win the lying game. You will lose.

DISHONEST SALES TACTICS

What we often think of as car salesmen lying is not always strictly lying. Often, car salesmen engage in manipulative ploys. Manipulative ploys need not involve lying, though they often do. Manipulative ploys always influence the other party's perception of the negotiation. The manipulator's goal is to appear to have more power than he does. And, perceptions of power are more important than actual power in determining the outcome of the negotiation.

Every manipulative ploy involves three steps: *dominance, shaping,* and *closing.* During the first part of the car sale, the salesman tries to dominate the initial relationship by shaping the sequence of events in an attempt to build value in the car. This period continues through the end of the test drive. Customers are not good at dominance and shaping because they are focused on the car, not on the relationship. Customers only focus on the relationship with the salesman once the price negotiation, (which results in the sale *closing,*) begins.

Here are a few manipulative ploys, only some of which involve the salesman lying. The important thing to note about each manipulative ploy is that if you, the customer, lie, it will *not* improve your situation.

BAIT AND SWITCH is what Monty did to my husband and me (in the story in Chapter Four.) First, the salesman paints you a beautiful picture of a great deal, then at the last minute he runs out of paint for any of a number of reasons. In order to keep the spirit and excitement of the purchase alive, you end up buying the more expensive package so that the salesman's pretty picture can be completed, framed, and delivered. A failed bait and switch is when you figure out what's going on, go storming out, and start all over again somewhere else.

In the tactic known as the **ADD-ON,** extra charges are added on to the advertised price, one by one, until the customer becomes uncomfortable. Actually, some amount of add-on is natural, such as in restaurants when tax and tip are added on to the tab. This means that customers have some tolerance for and even expectation of such extra charges. In every car sale, for example, taxes, tags, and freight charges are always added on to the "final" price. The car salesman is limited only by the boundaries of his creativity to dream up other elements that he can add to the price.

New car sales are *honestly* structured around the add-on tactic, not only in terms of adding charges to the basic cost of the car, but even in the way different salespeople are added on to the customer's experience. First comes the salesman, then the manager, then sometimes the general manager, then the finance manager, then the after-market girl. Then, the service and parts departments take over through the life of the car. Each car sale is segmented in this way so that the customer must argue with a fresh face, a face that is "innocent" to the previously negotiated charges. The add-on technique can be abused in that the salesman may add on false charges. Protect yourself by making sure you agree with each charge before another one is added on.

BRINKMANSHIP is defined as going to the *brink* of war without actually going into battle. Unfortunately, most car sales-men end up battling their customers, and then both sides must be fortified, rescued, or resuscitated by a sales manager. Car dealer-ship sales managers are the automotive-retail equivalent of Emer-gency Room doctors. Armed with psychic stethoscope, and an ample supply of deal-making instruments (ballpoint pens), they run from sale-in-progress to sale-in-progress, giving advice, yell-ing commands, and trying to keep their cool. They step in to take a sale's pulse, and have the authority to spend vast emotional and strategic resources to keep it alive, or to pronounce it as good as dead and send the buyers with declared deceased potential, rolling off the property upon the same wheels that delivered them to the battlefield. More often though, managers are calmly brought in to a deal-in-progress, routinely "dropping by" to "see how things are going." This is when Good Guy/Bad Guy happens.

GOOD GUY/BAD GUY: *"T.O."* is one of the first terms the green car salesman learns, because he is encouraged to do it, and does it often. *T.O.* means *turn over*. Salesmen *must not* let custom-ers leave *or* become too unhappy without turning the sale over to a manager. When the debate between the salesman and customer heats up, a manager approaches and introduces himself, whereup-on the salesman assumes the bad guy role, holding out for a higher price, or being difficult in some other way. The manager saves the deal by conceding to the customer, making the salesman look stu-pid, useless, and often at risk of being fired for his stupidity. Cus-tomers love to feel superior to their salesmen, so in any given deal, the manager takes over the deal and turns the poor salesman into a useless observer (that is how it is done: managers make the salesmen sit there and listen, but the salesmen are not allowed to speak). Most important in the good guy/bad guy ploy is that as often as not it is *real*, not staged. Salesmen and managers routinely try to humiliate one another in front of customers. For real.

Whether the humiliation and bantering is real or not, both salesman and manager appreciate that it is important for the customer to see that he has earned a higher caliber of assistance, that he is smart enough to have graduated from dealing with a dumb clerk to talking to the brains of the operation. Most salesmen I met performed the role of useless idiot quite readily. In fact, keeping salesmen feeling bad about themselves is useful for keeping their egos in check. Salesmen are constantly made to feel useless while being held to unrealistically high standards of performance. No matter how well they do, they are supposed to think they are losers. Compared to the way managers treat their salesmen, customers are kind and gentle. It takes a clever salesman indeed to work this system to his advantage.

One afternoon I appeared at the dealership for my shift, which started that day at 2 PM. I noticed immediately that one of the sales managers was strutting about with pride. He shot me a big smile as he walked by and announced that he could close deals that were unclosable, deals that nobody else could come *close* to closing. I believed him, since this particular manager, back when he had been a salesman, had the sales record to prove it. I wondered what had happened on this particular day, but considering the enormous egos that drive the car business, I had no doubt that I would find out soon enough.

About half an hour later, I noticed star salesman Henry Washington sitting at his desk, beaming like a lighthouse, and I knew the story involved him too. Henry has a special way of making customers feel like they are his allies. He leans across his desk so that his face is close to theirs, and speaks in a hushed tone, as though he is telling them privileged information, something of a clandestine nature. He keeps his head bowed down, looking into their eyes over the top of his black, thick-rimmed glasses. He speaks in a slightly strained voice, as though it hurts him to divulge what he is telling the customers.

On this afternoon however, Henry did not seem cool at all. As soon as I sat down across his desk from him, he sat up straight, and opened up like a spigot. Henry's story burst forth:

That morning, Henry told me, he had had a customer and had "earnestly" explained to her that he needed to bring stock in to the dealership, and that for every car he sold, the manufacturer would send him two more. He had made up numbers, announcing that he had 625 cars in stock, but he needed 1200. Of course, Henry told me, all of that is made up, but it worked to make this customer feel like an insider, as if Henry was revealing to her that *his* interests were to make the deal with her, even at a loss. The customer was close to making the deal, but wanted an additional discount. Henry told her that he would go get a manager to approve an additional discount, but that it had to be done a certain way: Henry and the customer would fool the manager. He instructed the customer to pretend that she had been to another dealership down the street; Henry told her the dealership's name and the name of the salesman who she should say had helped her. He instructed her to say that she had made a lower offer on the same car, again Henry told her how much the offer was for, and that the offer had been accepted. The customer was then supposed to announce that she was going to go buy that car, but that Henry had told her that he'd get in trouble if she left without first telling all this to a manager. The customer agreed to try Henry's scheme, visibly happy to be on the *inside* of a lie with a car salesman.

Henry trotted off to find the manager, and told him that he could not close the deal with this customer, and that the customer was about to walk out the door. The manager couldn't believe his ears: the great Henry Washington needed help, and was asking for it! The manager zipped over to Henry's desk and "took over" the negotiation. He spoke to the customer for a few minutes, bought her price-shopping story, and took $300 off the price she reported she settled on with the other dealership. The customer signed the paper. This is what Henry wanted all along, but he knew that the manager would yell at him if he made such a low deal all by himself.

The result of this scheme is that the manager thinks he closed a deal for the great Henry Washington, which he did, technically. The customer thinks she and Henry Washington took the manager for a ride, which they did. In the end, Henry came out on top by letting the customer think she controlled the manager, and by letting the manager think he controlled the customer. As Henry came to the end of his story, he leaned in closer, looked at me over his thick-rimmed glasses and whispered, "You have to work everyone."

Good Guy/Bad Guy can be a bit of a wild card because nobody really knows who gets to be good and who gets to be bad until they are knee-deep in it. In Henry Washington's story, the customer lied, but not *to* the salesman, and the deal could have gone bad. In the manipulative ploy known as **AGENCY**, it is necessarily the salesman who establishes a strong bond with the customer, and announces early on, without provocation, that he dislikes or even hates his tyrant of a manager, and that he is working for the customer, not the dealership. He explains that unless the customer buys, he doesn't get paid. In other words, the salesman is the good guy, and the manager is the bad guy, before there is any visible conflict, before the manager ever appears, *if* the manager ever appears. 'My manager is such a jerk. So greedy, always wants MORE! MORE! He tries to rip off the customer every time. I know better than he does that you're gonna buy a car somewhere else unless we give you the best deal. He doesn't care, he doesn't work on commission.' This last statement is technically true, however it is also misleading, since managers are paid based on overall sales. My general manager encouraged us to quietly point to him and curse him, in order to bond with the customer. 'Make me the bad guy. I can take it; I'm a big boy. Whatever it takes to sell a car.'

Even though *Agency* is a great tactic, in many cases it also happens to be genuine. The customer never knows, but the odd thing is that neither do the salesmen, until the sale is underway. The reason for this uncertainty all has to do with big money, quotas that change on a daily basis, and only the general manager really knows the true bottom line on any one sale. It is as though salesmen are improvising; they know the general dimensions of the characters they play, but they don't know where the script is leading or when it will end. Henry Washington plays *Agency* well because he really *does* resent all the managers.

HOW SALESMEN UNCOVER THE TRUTH

Car salesmen stereotype customers all the time. This is common practice, but it is tricky. Each customer is of course full of surprises, those that defy all stereotyping. Car buyers' preferences for car make and model may be predicted using general demographic attributes such as gender, race, age, family size, travel patterns, essentially all of the things the customer is *not* reluctant to tell his salesman. But there is another category of information that tells more about *how customers want to buy what they want*. Scholars at the MIT Car Project have postulated the theory that people buy cars at transition points in their lives, rather than during stable times. These transition events include marriage, divorce, birth, death, new job, moving, kids leaving home, increased income, or unstated personal crisis of some kind.

From the salesman's perspective, people arrive at car dealerships both as members of their general demographic, but also, often, triggered by one of these transition events. Figuring out which trigger, and which transition, helps the salesman guide the customer through the transition, and makes the car purchase a positive part of that transition. Customers think they are fulfilling their practical needs by purchasing a car, but salesmen are the bellhops to the often-heavy baggage that comes along to the dealership. And every suitcase is an objection that must be handled with great care since the contents can be extremely fragile. Sometimes, even often, car salesmen are honest, sensitive people who help their customers. I have seen this happen many times.

CUSTOMERS THINK IT IS ALRIGHT TO LIE

Customers arrive at the dealership heavy with self-righteousness. This is a problem for any commercial transaction since the salesman, right or wrong, good or evil, normally picks up on it, and then everybody's behavior is thrown into overdrive. The puritanical strain in many an American car buying customer is used to fight against his own desire for the car, at the same time that it is used to fight for a rock-bottom price, which is winning, not just acquiring, the object of desire. The goal, in many customers' minds, is not to find a price *that both sides can live with*; it is all about getting to *the truth,* and from the truth the "right price" will be revealed. That is the goal, and in the customer's mind, lying is justified means for achieving this goal.

Here is the typical scenario: The customer is in love with his future car. He feels that all of his research, thinking and test-driving of cars are a quest for truth, the true, right, fair price of the car he loves. But come time to negotiate, the customer is destabilized. He loves the car, but he also loves his money, though he does not realize how much he loves his money until the dollars glare up at him from the new car sale paperwork. The customer is faced with the salesman, no longer chaperone to romance, but instead the barrier to his owning the car. So, the customer convinces himself that only tenacity, rough negotiating tactics and even lying will win him his just reward. Of course, buying a car is not an epic tale of heroism, but without the perceived heroism, his "prize" is just a rather expensive spoil of modern American life, an unnecessary and frivolous consumer item, or worse, a necessity for which he has to work harder than he feels he should and for which he does not want to think he has struggled. To struggle for a necessity would reflect his lack of sufficient means, and to fight for a luxury item is regarded as petty. So, we Americans overcome our puritanical strain by giving ourselves *cause* to fight, as purists, for justice and fair commerce. Buyers tell themselves they are *entitled to* lie, even though lying does *not* help them get a better deal.

LYING IS A GAMBLE WITH POOR ODDS

When a customer enters a dealership with a number, say a thousand dollars below invoice, on a piece of paper, and says, 'We got this price at another dealership,' it is certainly a lie. What's a salesman to do? Sometimes salesmen will tell the customer, "OK, go buy it down the road for that price... bye bye now." But if the salesman does that, the customer surely will get embarrassed and leave the dealership. So, there are alternatives, and since the salesman knows that the customer started out by delivering a lie, he is completely invested in lying back to this customer and taking as much of a profit as possible on the sale, which is actually not always the way salesmen approach any given deal. In response to the customer's lie, the salesman has all kinds of responses that allow the customer to save face and start fresh. But he might just as likely be disinterested in selling to this lying customer, in which case he might challenge the customer with a question, such as, 'Oh, who did you talk to there?' A salesman who knows he has been lied to by a customer would do this for kicks, and would enjoy seeing the customer squirm. For a customer, lying is a gamble with very poor odds.

One year, the National Automobile Dealers Association (NADA) held its annual convention in Las Vegas, and I was there to watch. Like the rest of the visitors to Las Vegas, thirty thousand car dealers flocked to the casinos. I made my way to the Mirage Hotel casino, since this was where Mitsubishi, maker of the Mitsubishi Mirage, would hold a reception later that evening. Card dealers and car dealers. Both draw players to their respective tables and play their particular games better than anybody else. Card dealers know just how much to help a novice so that the fresh player thinks he has an edge. And car dealers know just how much to play their salesmen with and against their customers so that the customer feels he has an ally, an agent, and a salesman all in one. And each one knows how to use this skill to keep his customers stuck to the game until all the cards are on the table and all the money is gone.

While I played, the games manager came around, encouraged the dealers and me, just as a car sales manager swings by, and looks in on deals at the car dealership. Luck was with me and I won my first seven hands in a row. Not being a routine card player, I was very focused, trying desperately to remember the conventions that govern betting on 15, 16, and 17. My face must have worn quite a strain, because the games manager thought I was counting cards. He thought I was playing a dishonest game. He thought I was cheating. I could tell by the way he tried to distract me. He asked me a lot of questions while I played. He would not shut up. The salesmen watched the inquisition, acutely aware of the games manager's attempt to break my very real winning streak at the Mirage Hotel casino.

I was not cheating at the Vegas casino, but the casino made sure I would lose my focus anyway. Car salesmen expect customers to lie. Expect to be treated as though you are lying, even when you are not lying. Car salesmen are simply playing the odds; most customers lie.

SEVENTH COMMANDMENT - TO DO

Imagine that you already negotiated a deal using the Eight Commandments in this book. Imagine how confident you would feel, confident in yourself, the research you did, your tenacity and your integrity. Imagining how this feeling will help you stick to the truth throughout the sale. If you believe that the Eight Commandments are a stronger tool than any one lie or trick, you will have all the confidence you need to negotiate a deal without telling a single lie.

Chapter Eight

EIGHTH COMMANDMENT: NEGOTIATE EVERY PART OF THE SALE

Buying a car can be a fair commercial experience if you remember one thing: The dealership makes a profit on each part of the car you buy. Customers normally have only one number in their heads: "dealer invoice." That is the price the dealer paid for the car, without any of the "stuff" that gets added on. It is good to know that so that you can ask the salesman to sell you the car at dealer invoice. Taxes, license plates, and freight are non-negotiable items. Just about everything else is negotiable. If you are buying floor mats, pin striping, mud guards, a CD player, extended warranty, and credit insurance, be aware that there are profits, sometimes staggering profits, built in to each component of the final car + accessories that you take home. You know from the Second Commandment (visit your bank) that all financing packages accrue huge profits to the dealership. So too with options and aftermarket. And why can't service contracts and parts be negotiable?

If you ask what "cost" is on each accessory, you can "anchor" the negotiation from there, (assuming the salesman tells you the truth. If he doesn't, a good rule of thumb is that all add-ons are somewhere between 25% and 45% profit). Then the salesman has to *pull* the price *up* from cost, instead of you having to *push* the price *down* from retail. Try to be realistic and settle on a final price of cost plus a "fair" profit. Be careful though, because if you choose to buy and install a less expensive accessory from another supplier, you might void your service warranty.

To negotiate a fair deal on a car, you need to know the fixed cost to the dealership. Dealerships, like any businesses, cannot stay in business if they sell their merchandise below cost. Most car buying guides instruct you to focus on a figure called "dealer invoice," which is slightly more than the dealership pays the manufacturer for the car. There is another figure called "dealer holdback." This is usually about two percent of dealer invoice, and it is the amount that manufacturers pay dealerships after the car is sold. Dealer holdback can range from zero to three or four percent, so do some research into this before you try to negotiate it off your deal. For all the elements of the sale that I coach you to *research*, you will find useful websites in the second appendix at the end of this book.

It is also useful if you know the difference between the salesman's and the dealership's opportunities to profit from various parts of the sale. This chapter divides these opportunities so that you know where *your* opportunities are, when you are negotiating.

ANATOMY OF A SALESMAN'S PAYCHECK

How hard a salesman tries to steer his customers towards a particular model or color depends on two things: first, what manufacturer to dealer incentives are being offered at any given moment, and second, how this particular salesman is trying to work the dealership "pay plan," or sales commission system. We will revisit manufacturer to dealer incentives later in the chapter. A dealership pay plan is very complicated, but you should understand its basic components so that you will understand your salesman's basic economic position and motivation. This explanation really answers the common question: How much money does a salesman make?

If you are interested in how much the salesman makes so that you can use that information in your negotiation, you are not going to find a satisfactory answer. While it is true that the salesman wants the highest commission possible, the higher truth is that at the end of the day, all the salesman tries to do is get the customer to leave with the car, at any price at all that's acceptable to the management and that won't get the salesman fired. It's that simple. In the vast majority of dealership situations, salesmen need to make many sales, at *any* price, not a few profitable sales, to make decent money.

One of the two basic elements of the pay plan is gross profit on the sale. If the car costs the dealership $15,000, for example, and the salesman sells it for $16,000, the salesman might see 25% of the $1,000 profit, or $250, on his paycheck. But, the dealership takes a cut, called a dealer pack, before the salesman gets his 25%. The pack at my dealership was almost $400. That brings the profit down to about $600, and 25% of that is $150. Not such a good deal. In addition, manufacturers hold back a percentage of the cost, called a "dealer holdback." Dealerships get this money from the manufacturer after the car is sold. Holdbacks vary by manufacturer, but ordinarily salesmen make no commission on the holdback.

The other element of the pay plan is the number of cars sold per month by each salesman. In order for a salesman to collect 25% of the profit on each sale, he has to sell at least some number, let's say 14 cars per month. Anything below that and he gets only 15% of the profit for each car sold. Once he sells a higher number, maybe 25 cars in a month, he might collect 30% of the profit for every car he sold that month.

This is a loser of a system because oftentimes customers buy cars under cost, meaning that salesmen would make no money at all. None. The saving element to this system is that salesmen, depending on the dealership, make a minimum of $50 per sale, and after 13 cars, the minimum rises to $100 per sale, retroactive to every sale. So, a twelve-car month is a $1200 paycheck. That's about $14,400 per year, for an often 70-hour workweek. Anything under that 12 cars a week pays the salesman a salary that is too depressing to even calculate. National average performance is in the neighborhood of ten cars per month. Salesmen, as a group, do not make money. Turnover in the business is so high because most salesmen lose money selling cars. Some dealerships have moved to salaries with no commission for salesmen, precisely because most salesmen do not make enough money under the commission structure to make a reasonable living.

But back to the pay plan. Other pieces of the pay plan lure salesmen into thinking that if they win enough individual sales contests, they'll make big money. Sometimes this is true; sometimes it is a mirage. There is a prize for top salesman of the month. This can be in the range of $3000, frequently awarded in the form of a Rolex watch. There is only one first prize, and often nothing to console the twenty-plus "losers." To foster some teamwork in the dealership, the top team wins a cash award, based on their total sales. There is money for customer satisfaction surveys, both when the customers return them, and for the highest ratings. All of these contests run by the calendar month, so on the first of each month, every salesman starts chasing the same pack of customers from the same starting line. This is somewhat demoralizing, since the "end of the month frenzy" (when many shoppers rightly believe they can negotiate better deals), is gone overnight and all the charts are wiped clean. Salesmen sell best when they're on a streak, so dealers have another program, a motivational jump-start that rewards salesmen for good sales performance during the first five days of the month. Manufacturers are always running incentives to sell cars that are selling poorly, or to sell certain cars with special low financing incentives. Where I worked, sales were brisk Saturday nights, but slow Saturday mornings, so management frequently offered

$25 for every customer whose phone appointment walked through the door before noon. Another $50 might be awarded if one of those appointments resulted in a sale.

"It depends." That is the true answer to the question: "How much money do car salesmen make selling a car?" Even with all of these incentive programs constantly weighing on the salesman's mind, it is next to impossible to figure out what any given commission might be until long after the dealership's sales numbers have been tallied at the end of the month.

Some salesmen never have to struggle to work the pay plan. These are the salesmen who can sell anything, anytime. For them, the money comes easily, and the biggest shock is how big the paychecks can be for doing something so easy and questionably moral... How can it be right for a person to make that much money? Henry Washington talks about his astonishment, at himself, for staying in the business:

"The money was so big. I would close deals, man, where the gross was like eight thousand dollars. I mean I'd go home, it's like, you know, how do you do this to a person? I would go home and tell my wife. I'd be up all night. I didn't want to come back. That's a zoo, that's a money machine: mmmmm, mmmmm, mmmmmm. Why would anybody want to do that? See, once you get past the humiliation, once you get past all that, you know, here I am. I'm used to making the six-figure income. I'm coming in here and I'm dealing with dirt balls [referring to the management]. I'm dealing with people who can't even speak the Queen's English, who pick buggers from their nose, that fart, that belch, in front of people. The most uncouth people in the world that have got egos *this* big, and they're *that* fragile, you're dealing with those kind of idiots. You say the wrong thing, they'll go off, they'll go off, they'll go *crazy*, you know? So I said I got to get around all this, just like customers, it's what I gotta do. I want to sell cars and stay out of their way, 'cause I don't want to hang out with them. I wouldn't invite 'em over to my house, you know? These guys, they're making enormous amounts of money, enormous sums of money. But these are the kind of people I don't want to be around."

Henry Washington is often top salesman among a salesforce of over twenty-five salesmen. When Henry Washington sells you a car and makes a killing on you, he is so smooth that you don't even know it. Most car salesmen are desperate and you can feel their desperation. Henry Washington is the exception.

ANATOMY OF DEALERSHIP PROFITS

Customers value money as much as salesmen do, but they are too preoccupied with salesmen's greed to recognize that some profits accrue to the dealership, not to the salesman. A veteran salesman:

> The consumer is educated now. They don't give you the opportunity to make money. They come in with a book, and the car costs seventeen five, and they offer you seventeen seven, it's not logic. These people are educated, yet they come and make an offer like that. They don't *care* whether you stay open. They don't *care* whether you make a living. They don't care. They just want to get the car as cheap as possible. Now any common business person knows that you can't spend seventeen five for a car and sell it for seventeen seven, make two hundred dollars, unless you're selling ten thousand cars a month, in order to pay the electric, pay you, pay everybody. So actually [new] selling cars is the small pie. The big pie is service and parts and used cars.

The next section of this chapter lists all of the areas in which dealerships profit on the sale of your car. It is worth returning to this section when you are getting ready to buy. List all the elements of your particular car sale. List what dealer price is, then try to find out what dealer cost is. Use the websites listed in the appendix in the back of this book. Even if end up paying the dealership only some of the profit they usually "take" from you, you will save a bundle of money.

(i) Financing: Buying Money to Buy a Car

The more financially strapped customers are used to feeling less in control of financial matters. Car dealerships capitalize on this widely known fact once these customers are "in the box." The *finance box* refers to the small, plain, often stained-walled office in which the customer sits and stares at the back of a big computer, while the finance "specialist" does something mysterious and complicated to make the car available to the customer, despite the customer's "financial situation." This part of the sale often confuses intelligent customers who have been wise to every trick so far. This is where the big profits are made. Asked to describe his previous position in my dealership, an ex-finance manager shook his head and said simply, "Lambs to the slaughter…"

As the economy tightens and car buyers become increasingly financially strapped, a growing percentage of car buyers will be officially "credit impaired." This trend has already sparked the *special finance* industry. Special finance is high risk, high interest financing for people who don't qualify for regular car financing, and it really is a booming business. Unlike regular car buyers, special finance customers worry most about qualifying for financing, being "accepted" as a customer by the dealership. Credit impaired customers are qualified first, based on the payments they can barely afford and then they are matched to a car. This is backwards compared to the classic sales model of customers choosing, driving, and then thinking about affordability.

To repeat the Second Commandment: The best way to avoid being victimized by the finance manager when you buy your car is to get a car loan from your bank or credit union, and then tell the dealership you have secured a loan already and are not interested in monthly payments, only in a sale price.

(ii) Profits from Used Car Sales and Trades

Car dealerships make a great share of their profits on used cars. A used car is a unique item, so nobody knows how much it is worth. A new car, on the other hand, has a well-publicized suggested retail price. Therefore, it is more difficult to negotiate for a new car. Since used car *salesmen* know more than most used car *customers*, they win most negotiations, and a dealership's used car department makes more money than its new car department.

If you are buying a used car, the Eighth Commandment is a hundred times more important because every part of a used car is unique. The engine, the alternator, the tires, the paint job… If you do not assess every piece of a used car, how can you know its value? You cannot. Unless you know cars, you need professional help buying a used car. A trusted mechanic can help you out, but a broker can also help tremendously with negotiations once the car passes the mechanic's inspection and you decide you want to buy it.

When an old car trade-in is part of the deal on a new car, the dealership literally buys the old car from the customer, but the price of the trade is often hidden so that the customer does not notice how little money he is getting for his old car. He is usually too excited about the new car to care that his old car is an important profit center for the dealership. It is wisest to get estimates on your old car long before you go to the dealership to buy your new car. In most cases, you can get more money for your used car if you sell it privately than if you "trade it in" to the dealership. Think about whether you will able to find a buyer, and whether you want to spend the effort to advertise and sell your car, with all that that entails.

(iii) Aftermarket Options

In Chapter Seven we saw the tactic known as the "add-on," in which new items, with associated prices, continue to appear before the grand total. The tactic bears reviewing: First comes the salesman, then the manager, then sometimes the general manager, then the finance manager, then the after-market girl. Then, the service and parts departments take over through the life of the car. Each car sale is segmented in this way so that the customer must argue with a fresh face, a face that is "innocent" to the previously negotiated charges. The add-on technique can be abused in that the salesman may add on false charges. Protect yourself by making sure you agree with each charge before another one is added on.

The "Aftermarket Girl" is usually a woman who tries to sell you options like sound systems, rustproofing, and fancy hubcaps. The important thing to note in this segment of the sale is that each item you buy is negotiable. Each item has a healthy profit built in to its price. If you are planning to buy one or more of these options, shop around before you go to the dealership so that you have some basis for comparison. If the aftermarket girl tells you that installing non-manufacturer options voids your car's warranty, ask to see that fact in writing. Often it is true, but not always and not for all options.

(iv) Full Disclosure

How do dealers decide at what price their cars should sell, really? From everything that I could gather, the price is set individually every time, in the perfect free market system that is the modern car dealership. The more haggling there is, the less constrained or regulated the market, and the more we truly do *not* know the negotiated price of any one car deal.

When a market operates so freely, it necessarily evolves through periods of radical distortion, and such distortions trigger regulatory or market adjustments. Today, there is a sticker on every new car, which is required by law. This "Monroney sticker" is named after a congressman who required it after World War II when the GIs were coming home and there was a shortage of cars. With a huge demand for cars, dealers were selling for three or four times what they paid for them. Eventually the dealers were required by federal law to display, on the vehicle, the manufacturer's suggested retail price (MSRP). However, dealers are free to display any other stickers they want, as well. So, today, you see additional stickers that list costs such as 'Dealer markup - $2000' though the language is more subtle: 'Dealer-installed pin striping - $400.' Then there are 'ADM,' Adjusted Dealer Markup, or 'Adjusted Market Value,' both of which mean dealer profit.

(v) Manufacturer-Dealer Incentives

Manufacturers offer dealerships incentive programs. These programs come in two varieties. The first is annual or monthly marketing programs, where they put so much weight in terms of promotional activity towards certain vehicle models. The second is known as special promotions, which is when the manufacturer decides, on an ad hoc basis, to try to move certain inventory. These two types of programs filter down to the dealers, and the dealers then invent creative ways to motivate salesmen.

The manufacturer has the upper hand. Dealers rely on manufacturers for their inventory, so whichever dealership is the most responsive to the manufacturer's marketing needs will end up with the fastest selling inventory the next time cars are shipped. This means that customers are often given incentives to buy a blue car instead of a green car, just because the manufacturer miscalculated and painted too many cars blue. There is no reason that you the customer cannot or should not ask about these incentives while buying a car. An incentive split between customer and dealership is better than a lost sale. *Ask* about manufacturer-to-dealer incentives, as well as other marketing programs. You have nothing to lose and a lot to gain.

(vi) Customer Satisfaction

With decreasing brand loyalty and fewer measurable differences between dealers, the dealership industry is becoming increasingly competitive. J.D. Power and Associates of Agoura Hills, California, designs and administers a series of customer satisfaction and car quality surveys for the automobile industry. The customer satisfaction survey does not rate the car; it rates the salesman's service during the sale. The specific rating referred to within dealerships is the "customer satisfaction index," or CSI. High CSI ratings are important to salesmen, but they are more important to dealers. Sales Manager Jimmy Jeffries:

"The perception of car sales goes back forty years, the way things used to be done, and it's changing now with CSI. So people always come and they've had one bad car experience. They've always been taken once, or they had a salesman that lied to them. That was before CSI was invented. Now that CSI is invented, it's changing around slowly. But still, people have the fear that they're paying too much and that you're lying to them. You know, they always live with that fear, stories they hear, the TV, and the movie perception of car salesmen and how they deal with that stuff. A lot of that stuff's been true, but it's changing now because of CSI. The manufacturer's philosophy is basically, like I told you in training, they don't care if you sell a thousand cars a month, they'd rather you sell one car a month and get good CSI than a thousand cars a month and get bad CSI." Jimmy goes on to explain how much CSI is worth to a dealership:

"If you… wanted to open up another dealership but your CSI was bad, the manufacturer wouldn't give you the franchise. You want to get inventory, you want to get special inventory, you need cars, you say, 'Help help help…' Well, you've got one guy [dealer] who's got good CSI here, you've got one guy [dealer] here whose got terrible CSI, who do you think they're going to give their inventory to? Now, me as a training manager, I've got to train the salesmen with the CSI in mind. The pay plan's all affected by CSI. Everything's affected by CSI now." *Let your car salesman know that* **you** *know how important CSI is.* It is one of the most important pieces of information you can share with your salesman.

Here is a true story illustrating just how seriously dealerships take CSI: While I worked as a car salesman, I pursued other professional activities as well, including an auto-industry consulting trip to California. During that trip, I met with somebody at J.D. Power and Associates in their Agoura Hills offices. The person with whom I met about a time-sensitive public policy issue, which was totally unrelated to my experiment as a car salesman, asked me to write a letter and fax it to (J.D.) Dave Power as soon as I got back to the east coast. I flew back east on that night's overnight flight, and went right to work at the dealership. During a slow period that morning, I sat down to draft the letter to Dave Power. One of the managers walked by and asked what I was doing. I told him that I was writing a fax to Dave Power. This was, I realize now, a very strange thing for a simple car salesperson to be doing. Silent alarm bells went off in the dealership, but I was oblivious.

Now, around that time, some car salesmen had been hinting to customers who had just bought cars, that if they returned the next month with completed customer satisfaction surveys, a free tankful of gas might just happen to be forthcoming. The implication in this suggestion was clearly illegal by customer satisfaction survey rules, but it, or something like it, was probably common practice in many dealerships. I didn't think twice about any connections between my fax to Dave Power, and the implied tank of gas bribe that occurred now and then at the dealership, and my open reputation as a student of car market regulation.

Although I didn't make the connection, the general manager or one of his watchdogs did. At exactly 1:30 PM that day, management called a sales meeting, exactly half an hour before we *always* had sales meetings. 1:30 PM sales meetings never happened. Sales meetings are so regular that a salesman can disappear right after the 9 AM meeting, and then reappear only at the 2 PM sales meeting, and nobody would blink (if he were selling lots of cars that month). But if that same salesman missed the 2 PM sales meeting, he would be chewed out, no exception. At this special 1:30 PM meeting, David the general manager explained to us that he knew what was going on, and that we could no longer bribe the customers with free gas in order to get them to return favorable CSI surveys. He held up a letter, a useless piece of paper really, since nobody could read it. He pointed to it and stated very authoritatively that this was dealership policy concerning customer satisfaction surveys, and that any behavior that strayed from that policy was not sanctioned by the dealership and would not be tolerated in the future.

The next day, I sold a car. The day after that, I was fired from the dealership for no apparent reason. Dealerships don't like boat rockers, real or perceived. CSI is very important. Let your salesman know you know.

Eighth Commandment - To Do:

• Before you go to the dealership, make a list of all the things you are going to buy. For example: car, custom paint job, CD player, rustproofing.

• Research and list dealer cost for each of these components of the sale. Calculate a fair profit on each component, then add up the component prices you think make up a fair deal. Remember that some items such as taxes, freight, and license plates are non-negotiable items containing no profit to the dealership.

• If you have no idea what might go on your list, go to a dealership for practice, (any dealership will do.) Look at the sticker on the car window. Study it. Bring your notebook and jot down every component of the price. Then go home and make up your own list.

EPILOGUE:

CAN YOU AVOID NEGOTIATING?

Americans are getting fed up with the compulsory negotiation in the retail car business, and they have supported, through their shopping behavior, three major agents of change: no-haggle dealerships, shopping over the internet, and the used car superstore.

The trend in fixed price car dealerships started with Saturn when General Motors carved out a niche of "trustworthy car dealers." Once customers trust their no-haggle Saturn salesmen, the salesmen use their reputation for honesty and integrity to drive profits up very high indeed. Why shouldn't Saturn's profit margins on all accessories and extended warranties be just as high as their profit on the car's purchase price? If I were General Motors' Saturn division, I really would be in orbit over the renamed, repackaged Oldsmobile, which is what the Saturn really is. (General Motors tweaked an Oldsmobile and called it something new and fresh, but it's still a plain old GM product.) Is this a trend fueled by disgust of price gauging, or by the loss of the need for the notorious negotiation-specific duel until death (of the salesman)? If such a duel is no longer needed by car buyers, can we safely assume that the car is losing its romantic character, its "prize" quality, that we Americans are going to have to find some other way to enjoy the satisfaction of "the hunt" and "the kill"?

Buying services, by contrast, negotiate transactions at somewhere in the neighborhood of two or three percent above dealer invoice. Now, does Saturn's markup sound like a gentleman's agreement or a rip-off? Some non-Saturn buyers keep their feet on earth and bargain dealers right down to dealer invoice. The no-haggle Saturn dealership, on a car costing the dealership $16,000, is taking in profits of roughly $1920, whereas a dealership would take about $480 in profits from the buyer using a buying service. If I were a Saturn dealer, I would be happy to refrain from haggling too!

The fixed, no haggle pricing strategy that launched Saturn into retail orbit and which was mainly unsuccessfully copied by over a thousand other dealerships is not in itself a successful strategy. It was trickier than that. Saturn's careful dealership franchising plan is also responsible for its success. Most dealerships compete with several others in the immediate vicinity. When General Motors launched Saturn, it avoided this "overdealer" problem by opening only a few Saturn dealerships spaced far apart from each other. The result: no competition from other Saturn dealerships "down the street" or "across town," so no convenient opportunity to price shop a Saturn against another Saturn. The illusion of "fairness" is preserved, and buyers who really just want to have a fair experience are insulated from their own inclination to drive two miles to save a hundred dollars on an identical car. However, not everybody values the "civilized" (or is it just dry?) transaction enough to forego choice and buy a Saturn by default. And for every person who buys a Saturn (at over 10% above dealer invoice) on principle, there could be, perhaps, five people who won't buy Saturn, also on principle. Used car superstores sell cars for fixed prices, so they are really no-haggle dealerships as well.

Overall though, the car dealership industry is moving towards a less intensive negotiating buying experience for the consumer. But, says Jimmy Jeffries, "It's too embedded in the culture of this country. It's going to take a while for it to change."

Internet shopping and buying services and conventional car

buying services are two other new car buying industries, and they work like this: Join up for a small fee and waltz into a participating dealership with a membership card authorizing you to buy a car at something like 3% over dealer invoice, which is not an impossible price to negotiate on one's own, but it still takes work. Problem is, membership in these services is often packaged with a lot of fine print requiring the shopper to purchase some accessories such as pinstripes or floor mats, at terribly inflated prices to be sure. Buying services are simply institutionalized salesmen who work on contract with many dealerships and offer their members, their "customers," one take-it-or-leave-it deal. If you hire a buying service, make sure it is independent; that is, it does not work for any dealership.

In the end, the proliferation of the superstore, the internet, and contract shopping services is not unique to the car business. We focus on the "revolution" in consumers' disgust with traditional dealerships, when really, car retailing is changing at the same rate, or possibly even more slowly, than the rest of internet-crazy, superstore-crazy retail America. There are so many ways that consumers and legislators could regulate the car dealership industry, if it really wanted to. Americans will only lose our despised negotiation-based car dealerships when we grow out of our romance with driving, buying, and owning cars.

APPENDIX A - NEGOTIATION

Negotiation is more art than science. It takes experience, dedication, and intelligence to be a good negotiator, but it also takes creativity and imagination- that's because each technique is appropriate in only a small percentage of situations. How do you know what strategy to use in each situation? There is no one answer to that question. Instead, if you stick to the Eight Commandments in this book, you *will not need to* be a "strategizing" negotiator. This goes against the grain of most other car buying advice books, but the reality is that if you follow the Eight Commandments, you will already be most of the way toward getting a fair deal on a car, and you *will not need to* strategize.

However, there are a few tips that might make you feel more secure in the negotiating part of the sale. These are small but important elements. They are mainly reiterations and extensions of the Eight Commandments, but they are presented here as specific "tactics" to use during the negotiation. They sound simple because they are. They also work.

Focus on Price: Know ahead of time how much you are willing to pay for the car you want to buy, and for each accessory you plan to buy along with it. Stay focused on the price; do not let the car salesperson talk you into negotiating based on trade-in value or on monthly payments.

"Drop Anchor": Start the negotiation by mentioning a price that is lower than you are willing to pay. This "anchors" the negotiation at that low price. It is always best to start a negotiation at a low price and let the salesman bring it higher than to start with his high price, which requires you to bring it down. Do not make your anchor price insultingly low, or your salesman will get (justifiably) angry or laugh at you, neither of which are in your best interest.

Sit Next to the Salesman: As strange as this sounds, you create a more positive dynamic when you are literally on the same side of the table as the salesman. Psychologically, this gets the salesman, and you, to feel as though you are "on the same side" of the deal… which is the side that wants it to result in a sale! If your salesman asks you why you want to sit beside him, just tell him that you want to read the numbers he is writing as he writes them, instead of having to wait until he turns the papers around for you to look at. This is a plausible explanation, and one he will have a hard time refuting politely.

Be Respectful: Even if you don't feel it, show your salesman respect. You do not know for sure that he is a bad guy, so treat him like a good guy. If at any time you obtain absolute proof that he is a lying scoundrel, you will have the opportunity to leave the dealership and do business at another dealership. This will punish him since he will catch hell from his manager for "letting" you leave. As long as you are trying to make a deal, show respect. Showing respect goes a long way toward getting what you want.

Stay Positive: Once either side in the negotiation starts to be combative, things only get worse. If your salesman is combative from the start, ask the manager for a more positive salesman. The manager will, without a doubt, get you another salesman if you insist on it. All *you* have to worry about is how you are going to keep yourself from fighting with a positive, cheerful salesman who you think might be lying to you. If you can't stay positive under these circumstances, go to another dealership. At all costs, do *not* have a yelling match with your salesman. Even if you end up with a good price on the car, you will feel stress when you are in your car. It is not worth it. Stay positive.

APPENDIX B - RESOURCE GUIDE

This book is not an instruction manual. It has not guided you through every step along the way to securing financing, or to finding the appropriate sales channel for your used car, or how to determine how much your used car is worth. There is a wealth of information on how to find out these and many more critical pieces of information. You do need a lot of information to prepare yourself for your car dealership visit. Much of this information is free and on the internet. Here are some useful websites, by topic.

NEW CAR REVIEWS AND SPECIFICATIONS

Many sites review cars. Here are some of the most popular and complete sites:
www.caranddriver.com/default.asp?section_id=10
www.autosite.com/Reviews/default.asp
www.autochoiceadvisor.com

NEW CAR PRICES

Look up new car prices in these reference guides:
www.kelleybluebook.com (www.kbb.com)
www.nadaguides.com
www.carprices.com
www.automotive.com
www.theautochannel.com
www.edmunds.com (MSRP, dealer invoice, build our own car with options)

www.cars.com (online classifieds, build a car, see invoice prices—then request dealer price quotes in local area)

www.consumerreports.org (has many services on a fee for service basis, including finding dealer invoice, manufacturer to dealer incentives by region of the country, and dealer holdback figures).

www.cartalk.com/content/testdrives (test drive notes by the guys who host the radio show Cartalk)

RESALE VALUE – TRADE-INS

To determine the trade-in value of your old car, either at a dealership or through a private sale, try these websites:

www.nadaguides.com

www.kelleybluebook.com (www.kbb.com)

www.carprices.com (locate used car inventory by zip code)

TECHNICAL, ENVIRONMENTAL, AND SAFETY ISSUES

Check the fuel economy and average annual fuel cost of any car by year, make and model:

www.fueleconomy.gov

If you are shopping for a used car, check this site for complaints, defect investigations, safety recalls, and service bulletins on all types of cars and car-related equipment:

www-odi.nhtsa.dot.gov/cars/problems/tsb/

"Lemon Laws": If your new car is a "lemon," learn under what conditions you can return it to the dealership:

www.autopedia.com/html/HotLinks_Lemon2.html

The Insurance Institute for Highway Safety is a nonprofit research and communications organization funded by auto insurers. They publish vehicle crash test results:

www.iihs.org/vehicle_ratings/ratings.htm

CARFAX will tell you *what it knows* about the used car you want to buy; whether it is a lemon, or has troubling service records, or has ever been recalled. Just type in the Vehicle Identification Number (VIN). All this is under "free services" at the bottom of the page:

www.carfax.com

State driving laws, by state:

www.statedrivinglaw.com

CAR BROKERS / BUYING SERVICES

If, after reading this book, you still do not feel confident that you can negotiate a fair deal on a car by yourself, you can always hire a broker to do it for you. Expect to pay a few hundred dollars for a broker's service. Cost can exceed $1000, depending on what services are included (negotiating on car, obtaining financing, delivering car to customer's home, etc). Beware of brokers who take commissions from car dealerships. They do not have your best interest in mind. Brokers should charge a flat fee, agreed upon before they start working for you. Membership clubs such as AAA often offer car buying services, either free of charge or at low cost to buyers.

www.auto-broker.com (A nationwide car buyer's broker. $295 flat fee.)

www.carbargains.org CarBargains gets a least 5 dealers in a customer's area to bid on the make model and style of the vehicle desired.

www.costcoauto.com (for Costco members only. Dealers in Costco's auto program have agreed to charge buyers a price, usually somewhere between MSRP and dealer invoice. You should be able to get this price without Costco's help.)

www.aaa.com AAA has a similar program to Costco: Authorized dealers sell cars at AAA member price. No negotiation. It is up to you to decide whether this price is the best you can find.

FIND A DEALERSHIP - BY CAR MAKE, ZIP CODE

www.automotive.com

FINANCING – CAR LOANS

For an introduction to financing a car loan, see:
http://auto.howstuffworks.com/car-financing.htm

Membership organizations such as AAA offer car loans to members:
www.aaa.com (AAA car loan. AAA membership required. Apply online.)

CREDIT UNIONS

Credit unions are usually the best option for getting a car loan. Credit unions are nonprofit, cooperative financial institutions owned and run by their members. They are democratically controlled institution that provides their members with a safe place to save and borrow money at rates that are usually lower than bank rates or other commercial institution loan rates. However, you need to be a member in order to get a car loan from a credit union. Many employers, unions, and community organizations have credit unions. To find lists of credit unions in the United States, search these websites:

www.ncua.gov/indexdata.html (National Credit Union Association)

www.cuna.org/cuna/lg_roster.html (Find your State Credit Union League)

www.creditunion.coop (Lists several ways to determine whether you are eligible to join a local credit union:)

1. Call your state league. A representative will tell you about credit unions in your area that you are eligible to join. There is a list of contacts in each state:

www.creditunion.coop/statej_o.html

2. Ask your boss. Your company may sponsor a credit union, or may be a select employee group (SEG) that has access to a credit union. Many employers offer direct deposit of payroll to your credit union.

3. Poll your family. Does your spouse's employer sponsor a credit union? Most credit unions allow credit union members' families to join. Each credit union, however, may define "family" differently. At some, only members of your immediate family are eligible. At other credit unions, family may include extended family members, such as cousins, uncles, and aunts.

4. Quiz the neighbors. Some credit unions have a "community" field of membership, serving a region defined by geography

rather than by employment or some other association.

5. Read the yellow pages. Some credit unions rarely advertise, so you might not know about them unless you look them up. A yellow pages display ad may state a credit union's field of membership.

6. Call The Credit Union National Association. They can help you find a credit union by calling (800) 358-5710. You'll hear an electronic message that includes the name and telephone number of a person at the credit union league in your state who can help you find a credit union to join.

7. Check the online database of credit unions. Use the credit union locator.

LOAN CALCULATORS

Use these calculators to determine your monthly car loan payments. Enter the loan's interest rate, principal, and term.

These are two excellent all-around calculators, considering trade-in value of old car, outstanding loan balance on old car, purchase price of new car, cash rebate on new car given by dealer, sales tax, down payment, loan rate, and term of loan:

www.householdauto.com/java/eHouseAuto.html
www.aba.com/aba/cgi-bin/autoNT.pl

www.auto-loan-payment-calculator.biz/loan_payments.htm

www.bankrate.com/brm/popcalc2.asp

MISCELLANEOUS TIPS

1- Set up a free email account to receive feedback from website services. After you buy a car, cancel the account and the emails stop! Free email accounts are available at yahoo.com and other service providers.

APPENDIX C - TO DO LIST

Do all of these things before you go to the car dealership to buy a car:

♦ Buy this book and read the whole thing!

♦ Have a general idea of the car you want to buy, but be flexible.

♦ See if you can join a credit union. If so, join. If not, make an appointment with your personal banker.

♦ Ask your credit union officer or banker to explain to you what it would cost you, up front and over time, to:

1. Buy the car outright, with cash, if you can afford it;

2. Get a loan from your bank to buy the car, either a traditional loan or one with a balloon payment at the end;

3. Take the dealership loan advertised in your local newspaper;

4. Lease the car. You need to know the lease term, the monthly payments, and your options at the end of the leasing term.

♦ Dream about your car. Get brochures. Look at websites. Do a test drive at a dealership where you are absolutely sure you will not buy the car. ENJOY the idea that you will soon have a beautiful new car. This is a very important step. *Do **not** skip it.*

♦ Make a list of all the dealerships (and their hours of business) that could possibly sell you the car you want. Decide how far you are willing to travel to buy this car. Having a list of more than one dealership will make you feel as though you can walk away if you are treated very poorly at any one dealership.

♦ Buy a notebook. Start writing down anything you learn about the car you want to buy, and where you read it or heard it. Put your list of dealerships in this notebook. Keep your notebook handy- it's your friend!

♦ DO NOTHING about the salesman you are going to meet. Do not give him or her another thought. Do not try to understand what makes your car salesman tick. It does not matter and it will only distract you from getting the best deal you can get.

♦ Imagine that you already negotiated a deal using the Eight Commandments in this book. Imagine how confident you would feel, confident in yourself, the research you did, your tenacity and your integrity. Imagining how this will feel will help you stick to the truth throughout the sale. If you believe that the Eight Commandments are a stronger tool than any one lie or trick, you will have all the confidence you need to negotiate a deal without telling a single lie.

♦ Before you go to the dealership, make a list of all the things you are going to buy. For example: car, custom paint job, CD player, rustproofing.

♦ Research and list dealer cost for each of these components of the sale. Calculate a fair profit on each component, then add up the component prices you think make up a fair deal. Remember that some items such as taxes, freight, and license plates are non-negotiable items containing no profit to the dealership.

♦ If you have no idea what might go on your list, go to a dealership for practice, (any dealership will do.) Look at the sticker on the car window. Study it. Bring your notebook and jot down every component of the price. Then go home and make up your own list.

All of this takes work, but it's worth it. Saving a few thousand dollars is worth a few hours of work. If you agree, do these things. Follow the Eight Commandments!

Index

Notes

Notes

Notes

The Car Buyer's Bible

Featuring the Eight Commandments

for Buying a Car

ROBIN SEGAL, PH.D.

To order over the internet:

www.atlasbooks.com

To order by phone:
1-800-BOOK-LOG
(800) 266-5564

Call, Write or Email
Murray Hill Books LLC for

Large Quantity Orders:

212 689-5232

info@murrayhillbooks.com

Book Mail Order Form

Name: _____

Address: _____

City: _____ State: _____ Zip: _____

Email: _____ Phone: _____

Credit Card #: _____ Exp Date: _____

(Please note if card name&address differs from ship-to name&address)

Mail this form to:
Murray Hill Books, LLC
220 Madison Avenue
Suite 10H
New York, NY 10016

ISBN 0-9719697-4-4
LCCN: 2004117428

Number of Copies__

@ **$14.95** each = $___

Shipping @$2.95/order (up to 4 c

= $ _____

Sales Tax (in NY only): $___

Total: $_____

Signature: _____